For Reed Porter

Keep it moving!

573-286-5147

Fighting the Current
There & Back

In memory of my little brother Tony,
All who knew him will miss him.

Contents

Chapter 1

Before The Journey

I was working with a guy named John, when I first heard about Robert Carpenter's plans of an extended canoe trip. John had planned to join Robert, but had too many responsibilities at home. He told Robert that I might be interested and arranged for a time for us to meet.

After work, I drove straight over to Robert's house where he asked, "You want to try and break the record for the longest canoe journey?"

Without thinking twice, I responded, "You're not going without me."

I was born February 28, 1974, in Norton, Kansas. When I was two, my parents, Larry and Julia, moved me to Kansas City for my dad's job. My dad, being a truck driver, had traveling in his blood. Family vacations usually involved traveling cross-county via the family car and visiting the family farm located 7 miles east of Norton, Kansas.

My dad would drive hundreds of miles out of the way of our destination so we could see "the beautiful side of America." His favorite saying while traveling was, "Don't make me pull over!" and "There's nowhere more beautiful than America. There's no reason to go anywhere else!"

Walking across wooden planks that spanned the bubbling mud pools of Yellowstone National Park were my first memories of traveling with the family. Most of my playtime growing up was spent either in the "woods" or along the area's lakes and rivers.

Some of my favorite childhood memories were of hanging out on the banks of the Kansas River, where we spent leisure time throughout my youth. Somewhere during this time my parents told me how the water from the Kansas River went all the way to the ocean. My addiction to the outdoors and travel could not be attributed more to anyone other than my family.

After high school, I attended an automotive trade school in Phoenix, Arizona. Returning to Kansas, I worked in a garage for a while and then joined the U.S. Navy. That journey took me thousands of miles from home to the Persian Gulf and before it was over, I had circled the earth and visited several countries along the way.

Finished with the Navy, I attended college briefly before going to work in construction. The job kept me in good physical shape and financially allowed me to take fishing trips to Canada, paddle Ozark streams, go hunting and whatever else I could find to do in the Great Outdoors. Everybody that knew me, knew of my love of the outdoors.

Chapter 2

Preparing

From the very beginning, we planned to beat the record of 13,028 miles. The record was set by Neil Armstrong and Chris Maguiret in 1996. They had broken the previous record by tracing the route of Don and Dana Starkell. They had paddled 12,181 miles from Winnipeg, Canada to the mouth of the Amazon River, from 1980-1982.

It would take a long time to accomplish this feat, and we knew a lot of work was cut out for us. It would cost more money than we had and take two or more years to complete.

Neither of us was independently wealthy. Thus, Robert sold everything, put all his savings into checking, and moved back home with his parents to save more money. I started putting in all the overtime I could. However, the trip would still require more funding, and we needed sponsors.

For months, we worked at getting sponsors, grants, anything to help us along on this trip. Many companies were contacted, but there were no takers. Most companies replied that they did not give money for sponsorship and those that did, were sponsoring well-established athletes. Some companies laughed and said it was impossible. Some even went so far as to try to talk us out of trying. No one ever sent a formal letter denying sponsorship, they just didn't reply at all.

The most memorable denial was from a major canoe manufacturer who advertised a grant called the "Endurance Grant". It was created to support a longer expedition with up to $5000 in gear. During two phone conversations, we were given two reasons for denial. First, "We're leaning away from canoe manufacturing and leaning towards kayaks." And second, "The journey was *too* long."

Sponsors or no sponsors, the expedition would happen even if it meant we had to work along the way.

The next obstacle was getting support in general. No one took us seriously. Our friends told us that it was impossible to break the record, and only a few really believed we would actually attempt to do it.

Robert's parents were not fans of the idea. His father thought it would be best if we tried something shorter first, and his mother didn't want to hear about it at all. Like all good mothers, she was fearful of her son being out on dangerous rivers.

Planning the route was also a big hurdle. Robert purchased a few hundred dollars worth of topographical maps and began plotting the journey. He wanted to go further than the record, but not leave the United States. He wanted this to be an American canoe expedition, utilizing only rivers and water bodies inside our borders.

The date of departure was set for May 26, 2000. It was the Friday before Memorial Day, and we figured it would be easier for people to come see us off and not have to take time off from work.

Kansas City was the starting point; thus the first leg of the route would follow the Missouri River. There was so much to consider, like ocean currents, weather patterns, seasons, and of course, time. We could only go so far in a day.

Florida was the target when Robert first had the urge to leave in his canoe. However, with the record longer than originally thought, we needed more miles added to the journey. After careful thought and a lot of research, the plan was to make a figure eight throughout the continental United States.

The route was to follow the Missouri River to the Mississippi River, take the intra-coastal waterway to the Rio Grande and hopefully be in a warmer southern climate by the time winter arrived. Then we would navigate the southern U.S. and Mexican border and catch the spring run off on the Gila River crossing the desert southwest. At that point, we would portage to the Pacific Ocean and follow the coast north to winter in Northern California. Finally, we would follow the Lewis and Clark Trail back home to Kansas City.

After that, we would continue on to the Mississippi south again to the Gulf, this time circling the eastern states back down to Missouri. Then…who knows? This route would undergo many changes before the journey was complete.

The biggest difficulty to overcome was each other. Robert and I had only a passing knowledge of each other, we were not friends. Before this idea came about, we had only met a few times. We knew nothing of each other's strengths or weaknesses. Was the other capable? Reliable? Trustworthy? In an emergency, we didn't know how the other would respond.

To get to know each other better, Robert and I took a three day river trip near Rich Hill, Missouri. We put in on the Osage River (during flood stage) and paddled 60 miles to Monigaw Springs, Missouri. Afterwards, we were more certain about tackling a world record, but still had different opinions about what should be taken on the journey, and when those purchases should be made.

I made a list of everything I thought that would be needed for an expedition of this magnitude. Looking at the long list, I knew there was no way all of it was going to fit into a canoe. I shaved off what I considered "luxury" items—camp chair, sleeping pad, pillow, etc.—until I found the bare minimum: canoe, paddle, tent, and clothing.

When comparing products, I checked for durability, weight, size and price. I discovered, after visiting several of the local outdoor gear stores, that only a few of the employees had any actual knowledge of the products they were selling. Most of the advice they gave was read off the ad in their sales paper or from the item's packaging.

I decided the *best gear* for the trip would be products labeled: "pound for pound the toughest material" and/or "lightweight"; clothing labeled "waterproof and breathable", "quick dry" and/or "keeps its warming properties when wet."

My choice of canoe was lightweight, able to handle whitewater and carry more than 1,000 pounds. The only problem was getting it delivered. It was two months late, and the departure date was getting very close. Somewhere between the manufacturer and Kansas City, the canoe took an adventure of its own through the eastern states in the back of a box truck. Eighteen hours before departure, it finally arrived. Upon arrival, I discovered that it was damaged. A forklift had made a dent near the back of the canoe. The owner of the store shaved some money off the price tag to compensate for the trouble.

Robert already had most of his gear. He waited until the week before we departed to make any additional purchases. He already owned a recreational canoe and even though many advised him against it, he took it instead of buying an "expedition" canoe.

The biggest blow preparing for the expedition came only a month before we were to leave. Robert had contacted the world record book company over a year prior to departure about his plan to break the world record for the longest canoe journey. When they finally responded, the record was more than double what we had anticipated – the new record was 28,043 miles.

Neither of us had heard nor read anything about the new record during our research. We were surprised to find out that it was set back in the 1980's, long before the team of Armstrong and Maguiret set the record in 1996. The current record was held by Verlen Kruger and Steve Landick. They left from Red Rock Creek, Montana, April 29, 1980, and ended in Lansing, Michigan, December 15, 1983, after traveling all over the North American continent for a grand total of 28,043 miles.

It was hard to believe, and we were not sure of what to do. We had saved and planned for a 14,000 mile trek. I considered quitting right then and there, but with all the work we had done, neither of us could just walk away. This was a personal mission more than just a canoe trip. Whether we beat the record or not, we would go as far as we could and see what happened.

Chapter 3

Day of Departure

May 26, 2000

The forecast was dreadful for the day of departure. Storms, wind and hail were predicted for that afternoon. Our family and friends tried to persuade us to change the launch date until the weather was better.

Robert didn't plan on changing a thing. "We can't start running from the rain or we'll never get anywhere." Rain or shine we were going to launch. Everyone was shocked that we were leaving in the middle of a tornado watch.

Set to launch from Berkley Park, located on the south bank of the Missouri River in downtown Kansas City, the bridges were loaded with heavy commuter traffic coming in to the city to work. The enormous buildings of downtown towered above the park. It was a

18

good place to leave from because we were both from the Kansas City area. It felt symbolic to depart from this point, paddling downstream away from the hustle and bustle of the city, we knew traveling into the unknown, on a journey both of us had dreamed about.

Standing at the river's edge, a thousand thoughts ran through my head. I was a little nervous having never paddled the canoe I was loading. Its maiden voyage was going to be on one of the largest rivers in the nation. Many people had died on this dangerous and heavily trafficked waterway. The river was running high due to heavy rain upstream. In addition, Channel 5 news was there to see us off. It was the first day, and our first experience with media attention.

Several of my family members were there to see me off and show their support. With the exception of a few friends, Robert was alone. His father came down to the river to see him off, but had to leave for work before our actual departure.

© Photo courtesy of Julia Jellison

Around ten o'clock in the morning, we left in our canoes and started paddling away from Kansas City. Making miles was near effortless with the high water conditions. However, that ease came at a price. One of the storms that raised the water was fast approaching. After twenty miles of steady paddling, the sky began to darken. We decided it would be best to just pull over and set up camp.

We began setting up our tents just a little upstream from Missouri City on a wing-dam that we normally would never attempted to camp on. All the while, my weather radio repeated over and over to take cover, a tornado was spotted on the ground in the exact area we had set up camp.

When the storm hit, it hit hard. A large wall-cloud swept down the river and with it came 60-mile-per-hour winds, heavy rain and lightning striking the ground in every direction. The rain was so severe the bank began to wash away from below our feet.

Terrified, I abandoned my tent and curled up next to my canoe in the fetal position, praying to God that I didn't want to die. Between the roar of thunder and rain, I could hear Robert shouting. All I could see was the outline of his body, with his tent flattened around him. I believed the screams from his tent were of pain, but instead were of joy. He was having the time of his life.

As quick as it arrived, the storm began to break up. The sky opened up to sunshine, and two perfect rainbows arched over the river in the eastern sky. In the background, the storm crackled with all its fury, with lightening still striking the ground and the water around us. It was an amazing sight.

I later confessed to Robert that I had a long time fear of storms and lightening. When camping with my family as a kid, a tornado tore through our camp leaving us no place to hide but our camper. The trailer was lifted completely off the ground then set back down. Since then I wasn't a fan of being out in severe thunderstorms.

While we were settling in for the night, our families were worried sick. We originally were going to camp down river from Missouri City. Robert's brother, Ken, was waiting for us just downstream at a public boat ramp. Ken reported seeing gear and fragments of what could have been a boat floating in the rain-swelled current and feared the worst. They didn't know if we were caught in the tornado, swamped by the flood, stranded or worse, we could have been dead. No one rested easy until they saw us alive and well the next day.

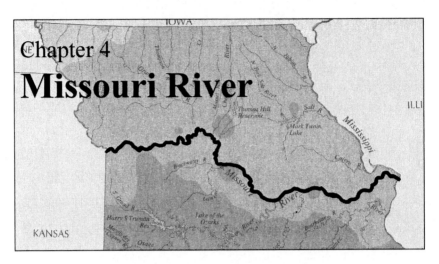

Chapter 4
Missouri River

May 26 – June 7, 2000

The morning after the storm, we awoke early, broke camp, loaded up and started paddling. We paddled past the historic Fort Osage, which could be seen from the river. This section of the Missouri River was terribly polluted. There was lots of foam on the surface and trash of all sorts: cans, bottles, fast food wrappers, tires, not to mention the pipes releasing foul smelling waste right into the river.

Long ago the Missouri River was formed high in the Rocky Mountains. Spring run off was channeled down the side of massive glaciers gouging deep into the landscape. After the glaciers receded, the river remained. The river spans hundreds of miles, from Three Forks, Montana, to St. Louis, Missouri, where it combines with the Mississippi River.

It was a dangerous river even for the large barges that traveled up and down its muddy current. Many eddies were marked with white crosses in remembrance of loved ones lost to the river. The high volume of water descending the Missouri pushed off the wing dams, creating massive whirlpools with intense undercurrents. The wing dams were built by the Army Corps of Engineers for flood control, and to keep the river navigable for barges and commerce. The river had swallowed up countless boats and barges. The sandbars and islands that used to line the entire length of the river were nearly nonexistent in modern times.

Despite the changes, it was still an amazing river. The power of it alone was mesmerizing. The high bluffs that lined portions of the lower Missouri River provided a sharp contrast to the tree covered surrounding hills. The sandbars were composed of fine textured sand, consisting of all types of stone found from Montana to Missouri.

The further we paddled from the city, the more the water quality improved. Most of the towns along the river utilized the river's resources for fishing, boating and skiing. The river people we met were hospitable and encouraging. Most wouldn't let us pass without telling the local news and sharing a couple of cold drinks.

In Glasgow, at the river's edge, several people were grilling burgers. Kenny, one of the locals, and his friends greeted Robert and I and invited us to join them for supper. Kenny had just lost his home and was living in the Glasgow City Park. There he had a permanent camp on the Missouri River. Morning, noon and night locals came by to give him supplies and to catch up on local gossip.

Lewis and Clark had also used Glasgow for one of their camps. Kenny was camped about a hundred yards from the huge petrified stumps that Lewis and Clark described in their journals. Robert and I made camp and toured the sites in the park.

PETRIFIED STUMPS
N 39° 13.185'
W 092° 50.841'

All day long, people were dropping by Kenny's camp, and every one of them was excited to meet the "canoers". A local offered to give Robert a ride to Wal-Mart to replace the tent that had been destroyed during the first night's storm. While with them, he toured the Glasgow Quarries, which supplied all the rock for repairing the levees washed away during the flood of 1993.

Back at camp, the group of visitors grew. Soon it was a party that lasted well into the night. Still, we rose early the next morning and were gone by sunrise. Robert gave his broken, storm smashed tent as a souvenir to one of the visitors.

According to our maps, there was a tiny little town nearby, and we were looking to replenish supplies, which hadn't quite dwindled, but provided an opportunity to re-supply.

On the north side of the river we noticed what looked like a boat ramp, and there was a large group of people gathered at the top. Without looking, Robert crossed over to the north side of the river, paddling towards the ramp and heard a deafening horn blow. He looked and from behind, a barge was about to run him over. Robert paddled as fast as he could as the captain got on the PA and started yelling at him.

Closing in on the boat ramp, several people began waving and hollering out, "Hurry! Hurry!"

We pulled the canoes up on the boat ramp and walked up to the top. It was shocking to see so many people with bicycles together out in the middle of nowhere. Two people were serving food from a van that had sponsors plastered all over the side. Everyone was wearing yellow and black spandex uniforms, and some of them were in wheel chairs. The cyclists began their trek in California 18 days prior and were meeting another team in St. Louis that had started on the East Coast.

The *Face of America* team was truly inspirational. To bicycle across half the U.S. in 18 days for anyone was impressive to say the least. Incredibly, some of these men and women were wheelchair bound and used hand bikes to travel.

The bicyclists immediately bombarded us with questions about what we were doing. A man approached us with a camera in one hand and a notepad in the other. He told us he was with the Outdoor Life Network (OLN) and wanted to ask some questions and take a few pictures.

After the interview, Robert and I were able to talk with some of the cyclists. The *Face of America* team

The river was now flowing parallel along the Katy Trail, which used to be a train track. The old MKT rails were torn out and the path was converted to the longest Rails-to-Trails project in the country. Over half the trail was along the Missouri River and followed along the Lewis and Clark Trail before it meandered through farmland.

was on a strict time schedule and soon, one by one, they rode off down the Katy Trail. Three members of the team took their turn with the support van and invited us to sit down and have a cheeseburger, at the local bar and grill near the riverbank.

MyLien was one of the people who was taking their turn as part of the support team. She had injured herself in a mountain bike accident and lost some of the use of her legs. Since her accident, she had focused a lot of her time and energy as a motivational speaker. The conversation I had with MyLien changed me. She had no bitterness of what happened to her and had only smiles and optimism of what lie ahead.

Darrell, another member of the group, was injured on a training mission in the military. Having no use of his legs did not stop him from biking across the country. Darrell inquired about the route we intended to take and noticed that we would be passing near Phoenix, Arizona, the following year. He insisted that we should give him a call when in the area.

Saying goodbye to the support team as they returned to their expedition duties, it began to rain. Waiting for the rain to subside, we stalled at the restaurant and had another cold drink before continuing down river.

The river began to change. There was anticipation about what was around the corner. For days there had been nothing but levees on both sides. Now a series of limestone bluffs, called Eagle Bluffs, lined the river. About 20 miles down from the bluffs, we paddled up to Sugar Loaf Rock, which was explored by William Clark on June 4th, 1804.

The tall rock stood alone like a monument. Lewis and Clark noted a natural arch near this location, which could be seen from the Katy Trail.

After Sugar Loaf, we were able to see the big dome of the Missouri Capitol building on the horizon as we paddled into Jefferson City. People were honking and waving at us as we passed under the Highway 54 Bridge. This was a trend throughout the journey, though we weren't used to all the attention yet.

Passing the mouth of the Osage River, we set up camp in sight of a power plant. That night, star gazing, a barge going up river shined their spotlight on us and left it for about a minute. It ruined our night vision, and we wished we had a marine radio to give them a piece of our mind.

The next day, we paddled down to the mouth of the Gasconade River, to Gasconade City, to meet up with John. He was our support team during this stretch in the Kansas City area and was bringing us supplies. After meeting with John and looking at the map, John wanted to meet again downstream about 7 miles in the town of Herman.

Robert and I pulled into Herman on the south side of the river, landing at the public boat ramp. We tied up the canoes as John drove up to meet us. The three of us walked together into the restored downtown district and had lunch at a nice restaurant.

Returning to the overloaded canoes after lunch, there was a small crowd gathered. Everyone was scratching their heads wondering what we were up to. They offered us cold drinks and asked if we needed any other help. Wanting to make more miles that day, we kept the visit short and paddled on.

Sliding the canoes back in the water, we told John we would call him from Washington, Missouri, just outside St. Louis. John asked us to slow down because he was still working on our website. We were disappointed that it still wasn't finished. He had promised the website would be up and running before we left on May 26th, but now there was little we could do from the river. John went back to Kansas City after promising it would be operational before reaching St. Louis. We paddled another 6 miles and set up camp on a sandbar island.

Clouds rolled in the next morning, providing relief from the brutal rays of the sun. We packed quickly and paddled on downstream. More recreational boaters could be seen on this section of the river. Jon boats, scarabs and jet ski's pulling tubers and knee-boarders were more prominent. Several different boats pulled up next to us and offered cold drinks.

Robert and I arrived at a small town in the late afternoon and re-supplied. The clouds were starting to get dark and we could see lightening in the distance. Paddling to the first flat spot we could find, we rushed to set up our tents and were ready for the storm to hit.

We stood on the riverbank in our rain gear and watched the storm roll in. Then we both retreated to Robert's oversized tent to wait out the storm. It rained so hard we could feel water flowing under the tent. After about an hour, the thunderstorm passed leaving a steady rain.

The next morning, we bailed several inches of water out of the canoes. It was seasonally cool and cloudy all day. We arrived in Washington around 4 o'clock and walked into town to make phone calls home. Robert tried to call John, but got no answer.

We set up camp on a huge sandbar that resembled a beach, covered with nearly white sand. The evening was spent planning our descent of the Mississippi River through St. Louis.

We woke-up around 8:30 and loaded our canoes. Downstream, we came upon a building located at the river's edge that looked like a prison, but it wasn't. We had never seen anything like it. There were no people in sight, but there were lots of cameras around the perimeter. A door was open and it looked like something off of a submarine with a big wheel to shut it tight. We guessed there must have been something valuable in there. We quickly paddled on downstream.

As we continued on, there were noticeably many more airplanes in the sky. At any given time, we could look up and see two or three. We were getting close to a city and could smell the difference.

Approaching St. Louis, we came upon a bridge being built. Fascinated by the operation, I took some pictures. As we passed under Interstate 70, the main interstate between St. Louis and Kansas City, Robert commented that straight down the road was home. It had taken us nearly two weeks to travel the distance, in which, a person could drive in four hours.

There was a big traffic jam on the bridge; a good reminder of what was left behind, and reaffirmed why we wouldn't go back for anything.

The following day, at Frontier Park in St. Charles we found replicas of the Lewis and Clark dugouts used by the Corps of Discovery. We also saw the Keelboats that were going to be used by the bicentennial Lewis & Clark re-enactors parked on boat trailers.

Despite the "Keep Off" sign, Robert climbed aboard. I stayed back at first, worried that we would get in trouble, but soon climbed aboard. The first noticeable thing that stood out was a throttle, for an inboard motor, which was kind of strange since they planned on going up the river the "old fashioned" way. Someone had put a lot of time into the beautiful craft.

Near Pelican Island, we made camp. Our planned route would lead us far from home, making this our last camp on the Missouri River for the next two years. This location was also the last campsite for Lewis and Clark's return trip home.

Two weeks into the journey, we had suffered excessively from sun exposure on the wide-open waters of the Missouri River. One thing not thought of, was sitting in a boat on the Missouri River, was like sitting in a frying pan; there was nowhere to run from the sun. Robert refused to wear a hat, leaving his bottom lip swollen and split down the middle. Attempting to eat or drink, he got blood in his food. His skin was peeling off in sheets, and his nose was crusted over from over exposure to the sun. I, on the other hand, wore a hat to protect my face, however, my feet looked like smoked turkey legs. In the words of One-Eyed Jack in Glasgow, "This River's a killer! I'm telling ya, a killer!"

Despite the physical ailments, the lower Missouri River was a great float. The river meandered through thickly wooded hills and bluffs, accented by huge fine-grain sandbars to camp on. Camping on these beautiful, ever changing articles of landscape was definitely a treat. Some of the finest sunrises and sunsets of the entire journey were viewed from the sandbars of the Missouri River. It was such a powerful experience that we were now addicted to the new lifestyle. The thought of quitting and going back to our old lives was something we never wanted to do.

The last day on the Missouri River, we took our time packing, being careful to balance the gear in our boats properly for the best performance. By the time we had departed, the hot summer sun was high in the sky, making the hours seem to pass by slowly.

We began to get hungry for lunch and started looking for a place to stop. I spotted a shady rock bank and we pulled over. While scouting the area, Robert climbed up a 15-foot rock cliff and found a small cave with cold running water. I had been looking for about a day for a place to fill my water jugs. After lunch, we took flashlights and Robert's video camera to explore the cave.

It had a small entrance, only about 2 ½ feet x 2 ½ feet and water filled the bottom 5 inches. Robert could see it opened up a little, so we went on in. The entrance was lined with mosquitoes and spiders as we crawled on our hands and knees through running water to an opening in the cave about 30 feet long, 10 feet wide, and 6 feet high. There were no formations or critters, but there were raccoon tracks and tiny freshwater shrimp. By the looks of an old rusty pipe, it appeared the cave was once a water supply. We filled our water jugs and moved on.

Paddling downstream looking for a place to call John, we had no luck. At the mouth of the Missouri River we saw two guys fishing from a boat. The fishermen waved us over and insisted on talking about the journey. Dutch, one of the men, asked if we needed anything and jokingly Robert said, "I broke my paddle."

Instantly, the other man jumped up and gave him two paddles. Dutch pointed out an island and said it would be a great place to camp. They gave us advice on how to navigate the Chain of Rocks rapids, and offered to wait at the bottom, to pick up our gear, if we wiped out.

We paddled out of the mouth of the Missouri River onto the wide-open waters of the muddy Mississippi River. At sunset, we landed on an island still in view of the Missouri River and set up camp on a beautiful sandy beach. The island was around 300 yards long, maybe 100 yards wide, and composed mostly of fine textured sand, perfect for walking around barefoot. A person could step out of their boat, onto the sand, without a worry of rocks or debris.

I did some fishing that night, but only caught gar that were 2 to 3 feet long. Robert filmed me with his video camera in one hand and a flashlight in the other, loosing a huge catfish at the bank. I fished until running out of bait around midnight.

A flock of geese hung out behind our camp all night long. Even though they made noise all night, the sound of the waves from the passing barges lulled us to sleep. The waves gave a feeling of sleeping next to the ocean.

The next day would be a tough one passing thru St. Louis on the Mississippi River.

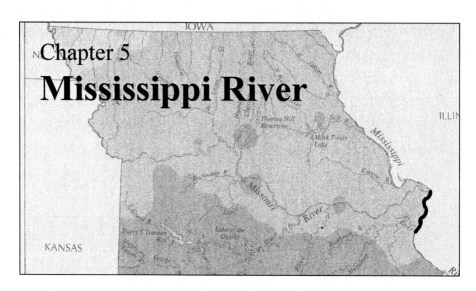

Chapter 5

Mississippi River

June 8, 2000

From the confluence, we had only a little over 30 miles of the Mississippi River to reach the mouth of the Meramec. First, we had to navigate through the Chain of Rocks. The Chain of Rocks consisted of boulders and debris that span the width of the Mississippi River creating dangerous rapids just below the confluence of the Missouri and Mississippi Rivers. Debris of all kinds—huge trees, tires, and trash—littered the way through.

We pulled over to scout a route through the rapids. There was a narrow shoot that appeared to have room for us to slip through. One mistake and we would become part of the debris pile or get caught in the strong undercurrents and possibly drown. There was only one possible route a canoe could go, and the little shoot was only four-feet wide. Directly at the bottom of the four-foot drop there were two logs sticking out of the water that we would have to dodge. To capsize there, we could die; or risk serious injury and wish we were dead. Failure to succeed would mean disaster and the end of the expedition.

I insisted on giving it a shot, wanting to put my new boat to the test. Robert thought it would be wiser to unload the canoes and portage around, since he only had a recreational canoe not made for whitewater. But if I was willing to try it, Robert was willing to try it, too. A man from the water department was talking on a handheld radio as he watched us prepare to run the rapid.

Paddling out into the swift current, I dropped into the huge rapid and managed to get through the narrow opening between two large logjams pinned against the boulders. I eddied out and watched Robert run the dangerous rapid without incident.

About a mile past the rapids, the US Coast Guard showed up to see if we needed help. It seemed they expected to be picking up our gear from the water. We kept paddling as the boat approached. Within about 75 feet of the canoes they started giving the thumbs up. The Coast Guard knew we had run the Chain of Rocks unscathed and were happy to see that the rapids hadn't taken us.

We continued downstream for another couple of hours to where the river became very congested. Several barges were coming up and down the river at the same time causing a traffic jam. Waves, sometimes three, even up to six feet tall, tossed us around threatening to swamp our open canoes. In addition, Robert and I were trying to keep from being sucked underneath the parked barges that were four deep lining the banks of the river. Stories of people being killed in this matter really got our attention.

Finally the Arch appeared in the distance, and we were shaking from adrenaline. It was like being on a roller coaster for 4 hours that we could not escape. The bank was lined with tourists and parked cars visiting the famous arch. There were hundreds of people everywhere. Pulling the canoes up onto the cobblestones beneath the arch, I went to use the phone. Robert sat and watched the boats until I returned.

Under the arch was a McDonald's built on a floating barge. Robert thought it was the best cheeseburger he'd had in a long time. We ate from the value menu until we couldn't eat anymore, then paddled off towards the Meramec River. The waves from the barges made us a little seasick, but we refused to let McDonald's come back up.

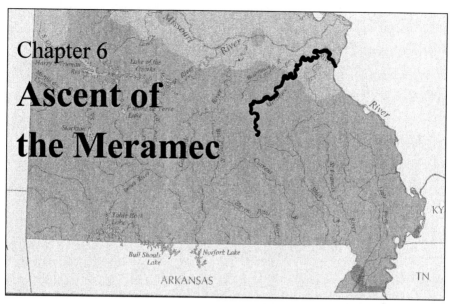

Chapter 6

Ascent of the Meramec

June 9 – July 12, 2000

The mouth of the Meramec River was only a few hours of paddling downstream from the St. Louis Arch. Determined to make it to the Meramec River, we pushed on and arrived late afternoon. The steep banks of the lower Meramec offered little opportunity for camping. We paddled several miles upstream and near sunset, spotted a boat ramp in front of a campground.

At a nearby trailer we met Curly, the owner, and told him our story. He allowed us to make camp at no charge near the water's edge. It had been a long stressful day and we were ready for some sleep.

Waking up after a good night of sleep, we climbed out of our tents into media frenzy. Some of Curly's friends had notified various news stations of our mission. That day we were interviewed by three of St Louis' major TV networks and a radio station. FOX even went as far as to fly their news helicopter over a staged paddle session of us climbing the Meramec.

That evening Curly sponsored a huge barbeque in our honor. Dozens of people attended the party. Just before the nightly news, he set up a TV outside and we all gathered around. Flipping through the channels, we heard a reporter say, "Down on the Meramec Live..." and the crowd went wild, followed by shushing so people could hear. It felt strange to have this much attention brought on us having only been on expedition for two weeks. Regardless, we felt proud to be able to share the moment with such a great group of people.

The next morning we decided to stay and rest another day. We met several interesting people during our stay at Curly's World. One gentleman was a chainsaw artist. Not even introducing himself, he pulled two cedar stumps from the back of his van and carved two wooden stools for us. After a quick handshake, the man packed up and drove away.

After all the excitement at Curly's World, we began our ascent of the bluff lined Meramec River. The current was calm and slow as we paddled up thru the suburbs of St Louis. Wave runners buzzed the width of the river, tormenting fishermen and other boaters.

About 30 minutes up river, the cowboy coffee hit Robert and he had to pull over. Robert quickly climbed the riverbank and found some bushes. After he got the hole dug and his pants down he heard, "Fore." He looked over and could see a group of gentlemen teeing off. He wanted to start laughing, but was afraid he would give away his position. He quietly did his business and came back down to the river where I was holding his canoe. Trying to keep from laughing, he said, "Man, you'll never guess what I just did. I just used the bushes on a golf course."

We laughed about it for about an hour afterwards as we paddled up the river.

After climbing a couple of miles of river, Robert noticed a splash between our canoes, which were about 10 feet apart. He looked at me and asked, "What the heck was that? Someone just shot or threw something at us."

We then heard laughter coming from a balcony full of partying college kids, high up on a nearby bluff. One of them yelled, "Almost got 'em!"

Robert turned to me and said, "Those punks just shot at us."

We were shocked because they were over a hundred yards away, quite a distance for something to be thrown. It had to have been shot, either by gun or sling shot, but we heard no sound indicating how.

Thinking about how the actions of those kids could have killed one of us or jeopardized the whole expedition by causing a severe injury, made Robert snap. He grabbed his rifle and screamed, "We're pulling over and taking this hill. We'll sneak up in the night."

I calmed him down and talked him out of it. He came to his senses and agreed, "Yeah, you're right. We shouldn't do anything. Let's just keep paddling."

Not long after the shooting incident, heavy unseasonably cool rain started to pour. We pulled into a boat launch and hung out talking with a family, while lightening flashed all around. Other boaters were pulling up and running to their cars and trucks, taking shelter from the storm.

Robert and I sat down on the riverbank to watch the show. After being in the elements so long we knew there was nowhere for us to hide. Some guys on wave-runners pulled up to sit out the storm with us. Earlier that day we had complained about reckless and inconsiderate people on wave-runners. Now we had ended up sitting out a storm with the very guys we had complained about and discovered they were pretty cool.

Paddling up river the following day, we were greeted by someone shouting down at us from atop a steep mud bank, "What are you boys doing down there!"

The tone of the question insinuated that we were trespassing. After explaining ourselves, Carlos invited us to stay a while and meet his friends. Climbing up the steep river bank, we spotted a small log cabin up on poles. At first glance, it looked like it had been there for over a hundred years. We were given a quick tour of the earthy smelling, rustic cabin before relaxing around their campfire.

Carlos had a camper trailer parked on the riverbank, and let us spend the night and use the shower. The next morning they sent us off with a case of coffee.

The following day, John from Kansas City and his son Nathan brought us some supplies. They spent the night with us on the riverbank near a primitive boat ramp. During the night, beavers slapped their tails letting everyone know whose territory we were in.

After saying goodbye the next morning, we got a late start. Father's Day was soon approaching and we hoped to be near a telephone in time to give our fathers a call.

Storms became a daily event on the Meramec. It had been a dry year and the local residents welcomed the rain. We weren't as enthusiastic paddling upstream, with the water on the rise. When large trees and limbs started coming down river, it became too dangerous to continue. Thus, we were forced to set up camp.

All day, we watched the river rise, slowly creeping foot by foot to the edge of camp. In the rain, we moved camp to even higher ground. For three days we were stranded and were unable to call home to wish our dads a Happy Father's Day. The river finally crested and began to clear, so we could continue our journey.

"You're going the wrong way!" was the common exclamation heard from people along the way as we were fighting the current. Most people thought we were plain crazy.

Several miles from the mouth of the Meramec, the river traffic started to taper off. Spotting a couple coming downriver, we waved to each other in passing. Further up, stopped for lunch, the man and woman came back up river.

"You're going the wrong way!" we told the couple.

They pulled over for a formal introduction and handshakes. Doug then pointed out a canoe submerged under water across the river and wondered if Robert or I knew who it belonged to.

Robert and I helped him retrieve the canoe, and it now belonged to Doug. Doug told us their place was just up river a couple of miles and invited us to a home cooked dinner, which we gladly accepted. Doug and Debbie continued on upstream.

At River Rat Camping and Canoeing, a local outfitter, we pulled our canoes up on the boat ramp and spotted a pop machine in front of the main office. We dug for change and walked up to get a soda and introduce ourselves. It was a small mom and pop, family owned campground and canoe outfitter just outside of St. Clair, Missouri. We spent some time with the owners sharing stories of the expedition.

We continued on up to Doug and Debbie's place on the river. After a home cooked meal, we stayed the night. Robert recorded their sons, Chad and Brodie, showing off their acrobatic skills. They were doing handstands, walking on their hands up and down the ramp from the deck to the driveway.

The next morning after breakfast, Chad and his friend Tim, took us on a tour of the property and found a few arrowheads. They had several acres along the Meramec River where Doug had built their home right into the side of a bluff. The back deck looked out over the river valley. In their yard was a huge shagbark hickory tree, recorded as the largest in the state of Missouri. Below the deck was a rock garden filled with Indian artifacts found on the property. A natural spring ran along the side of the house, down to the Meramec River. It was a beautiful home.

The following morning, Debbie took Robert and me to a grocery store in town so we could pick up some much needed supplies: food, batteries, etc. When we got back, Robert discovered his video camera had quit working, so he used the kitchen table to operate on it. He disassembled it and found moisture inside. He borrowed a hairdryer to dry it out, and got it working again.

By then we realized that Doug would be home from work in a couple of hours, so we decided to hang out another day and visit some more with our new friends. We were entertained by Debbie's stories of strength. She was able to roll a big bale of hay all by herself. Doug had great stories of his martial art instruction and dreamed of working missionary work abroad. A couple of years later, he did just that.

We got an early start the next morning with Doug and Debbie seeing us off at the riverbank. They insisted that we stay in contact

with them, and reminded us to explore Roaring Spring, which wasn't far up river.

In search of Roaring Spring, we encountered a tree that was directly in our path on the eddy side of the river. We had two choices: unload the canoes and portage around it, or pull out the machete and start chopping. I gladly started chopping away.

After several minutes of chopping, we realized it was home to thousands of tiny spiders and some of amazing size, up to 6-inches wide.

Robert's hand was covered with tiny spiders and he screamed like a little girl. He quickly brushed them off and made sure nothing was still crawling on him. I laughed as he took out his camera and recorded the "National Geographic" moment. We soon realized it would have been much easier to portage around, but we were having too much fun playing in the water with the spiders by then.

After chopping some limbs away, we passed the canoes through the downed tree and brushed the spiders off our seats. We paddled on and found the well-known Roaring Spring coming out of a cave. The beautiful, crystal clear blue stream of water was about 10 feet wide and two feet deep. We took a break and had lunch.

Two days later, as I was wading up a riffle, I was being stalked by a huge spider on the gravel bar next to me. Each time I looked over, the spider was moving closer to my location. I splashed water toward the spider in an attempt to scare it off - to no avail. The spider would just charge back at me. Finally, believing I was far enough from the spider to ignore it, I turned my back to it. At that moment, the spider closed the gap and launched nearly 4 feet skipping off the water and landing on the back of my calf. It was so large it completely covered the entire back of my calf.

I let out a loud scream and knocked the spider off the back of my leg. Thinking I had at the very least injured it, the spider stood its ground ready to attack again. When I had given Robert a hard time for screaming like a little girl when he had spiders on him, Robert had said, "We'll see how funny you think it is when it happens to you." Today was Robert's day, as he got the last laugh.

Now 500 miles into the journey, Robert and I arrived at Meramec Caverns and made camp. The caverns were a popular tourist attraction, and since we were there, we decided we'd portage to the cave entrance and take the tour before leaving the next day.

The next morning, an adventure scout group that had camped next to us shared a sausage, egg and cheese Dutch oven breakfast. It was awesome compared to my routine oatmeal for breakfast. After two helpings, the group offered the leftovers to take with us.

It would have been a perfect morning except for the constant moaning and dry-heaves of a hung-over man echoing throughout the campground. The sounds of the man's misery were in direct contrast to the sounds of laughter the night before, and continued on for over an hour. Finally he silenced while we were packing.

46

Saying our goodbyes to the scout group, we portaged a quarter mile toward the entrance of the cave. Before we reached the entrance, our portage carts collapsed forcing us to unload everything and reinforce the frames. We had been told that they were the best carts on the market, but we quickly found out they were junk. This was among the first major modifications that we made to our gear.

The cave was promoted as a Jesse James hideout and featured many colorful formations with various colored lights. It also had the only pendulum in the world that didn't work. The tour concluded, and we headed back to the river after checking in at home.

Along this stretch of river swimming was prohibited. There were big white signs lining the banks, warning the public of underwater caverns. Several people, including scuba divers, had lost their lives by being sucked into the caves never to be seen again.

We took the time to explore many of the caves that dot the dolomite bluffs along the river. Fisher Cave was one of the more interesting cave tours. Unlike most cave tours, this cave was not wired with electrical lighting. Each person was issued hand held lanterns at the mouth of the cave.

Towards the back of Fisher Cave, the naturalist guide pointed to a wall with bear claw scratches. These were another reminder of how man had drastically changed nature over the last 200 years. The guide also pointed out a cave formation that was unique to Fisher Cave. The formation defied physics and cave formations around the world. There were stalagmites with no stalactites. There was only one other place in the world like it. The Fisher Cave tour was rated as one of the best in the "cave" state.

A little up river from Meramec State Park, we paddled up to a cave entrance that began at the river and rose nearly 100 feet high. Green's Cave was its name, and it became our home for the next two days. While there, youth groups, college kids, and others came by and visited with us during our stay.

The second day at Green's Cave we were looking at our map, which was practically worthless after being wet so many times. Sitting in camp later that day, we joked about our worthless map, and laughed about not having one.

At that moment, a woman who was leading one of the youth groups walked up and said, "I noticed your maps were in shreds. Here, take mine."

She handed over a brand new Missouri topographic atlas. It had to be a miracle. For a few minutes she stayed and talked

with us. She was spending the summer guiding less fortunate children down Ozark streams. The sun was sinking fast and we thanked her once again while saying goodbye. The youth leader paddled away, heading downstream in her kayak.

The river began to clear the farther we traveled upstream. It was also swifter and much more shallow, making travel more difficult. Most of the time we waded through the water, pulling the canoes behind, as the occasional passer-by reminded us, "You're going the wrong way!"

At Garrison's Campground, Doug and Debbie showed up to celebrate Independence Day. Garrison's put on a fireworks show that lived up to its claim of being one of the "best in the state."

For a few days, Robert and I separated so he could spend time with a girl from back home, so I made a solo trip to Meramec Spring.

The spring was a sight to behold. Crystal clear water gushed up out of a cave, deep within the pool. Looking down through the water, I could see trout swimming in and out of the cave, fighting against the swift current. The area below the spring was designated a trophy trout and smallmouth bass fishing zone, with strict regulations.

After a few days, Robert paddled up to meet me and we hung out at Meramec Spring for a few days. There was a lot more to see than just the spring. There were several historic monuments representing the use of the spring over the years. An old cemetery overlooked the park with tombstones dating back well into the 1800s. Surrounding the trout fish hatchery, were ruins of an old mill and metal refinery. Meramec Spring, a National Scenic Monument, was a great fisherman and family friendly place to visit.

After restocking our food supplies, we continued up river. Above the spring, the stream had become a small creek. We passed under a bridge where a group of people were cooling off. One of them said they had seen us on TV in St. Louis and wished us good luck.

Since the beginning of the expedition, one thing was made perfectly clear to us: topographic maps were not 100% accurate. We were cussing mapmakers the whole way and joked that we would love to get our hands on one.

Further up the shallow creek, we found a small Hereford calf stuck in the riverbank. It was crying for its mother and looked like it had been there for a couple of days. I walked to the nearest farmhouse to find the owner and then led him to the helpless calf. The calf came out of the mud with ease, but a mud embankment still stood between the calf and its waiting mother. Since the embankment was too steep for the farmer, I took the calf from him and climbed the 15-foot bank as Robert pushed me from behind. I released the calf to its awaiting mother, who began to nurse her baby.

As we talked, the farmer told us that he used to be a mapmaker for the United States Geological Survey. He said that the USGS relies on people like us to report inaccuracies on the maps. Robert and I couldn't help but laugh, remembering our earlier comments about mapmakers.

Above Meramec Spring, the river was nearly unused except by the locals. With the river barely able to float our canoes, we were forced to wade in order to make any progress. The map showed a small country road where we could begin our portage to the Current River. Looking for that road, we came across a family of three eating along the river.

We told the father about our search for the country road. The man said, "You're here, but this is private property." After introducing ourselves and explaining our story, Phil thought we were lying. Finally, after convincing him of the authenticity of our story, his attitude and stature changed. He insisted we make camp on his place and gave permission to use the road.

Phil took us on a drive the next day to scout the route of our first long portage. After looking at several options, the route chosen was mostly over gravel roads, which offered shelter from the busy highways. After looking at the Ozark hills that had to be crossed, we concluded that the trip could be done over two days of walking.

After climbing 191 miles of the Meramec, we were itching for some downstream action. Only 33 miles of Ozark hills stood in the way.

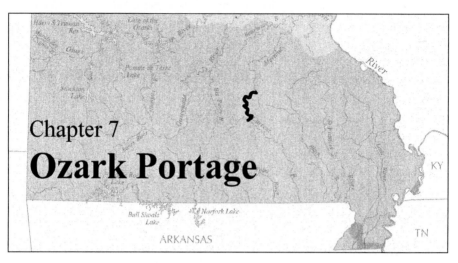

Chapter 7
Ozark Portage

July 12 – 16, 2000

R obert and I awoke at 3:00 a.m. after very little sleep to prepare for our portage from the Meramec to the Current River. Coffee was boiling on a propane stove, while we attached the portage carts to the center-bottom of the canoes. We packed all our belongings into the canoes, putting the heaviest items centered over the portage carts. The last items to be packed were placed in a manner to ensure the canoe was perfectly balanced. We each fabricated a harness and secured it to the bow of the canoe. This allowed us to pull the heavy loads, hands free.

Within an hour, we set off down a gravel road pulling the canoes with flashlights in hand. The early morning air was thick with fog, and I had to constantly wipe condensation from my glasses.

Eventually I took them off as we walked side by side down the Ozark gravel road.

Robert suddenly yelled, "Stop!" as he grabbed my arm pulling me backwards.

Only a foot away from my feet was a copperhead coiled up and ready to strike. We moved the snake off the road and continued portaging.

Just as the sun began to rise we reached the blacktop. We went past a charcoal factory, and some of the workers did a double take as Robert and I pulled our canoes along. The workers pointed and shook their heads. The fog slowly burned off as the sun rose higher, turning the beautiful morning into a hot sticky one.

We reached the next gravel road and took a break. Robert walked a quarter mile down the road to buy a six-pack of cold pop. A security guard just coming off his shift stopped and asked if we needed a ride. For about 15 minutes we talked about the expedition. Before the guard left, he signed our witness book.

Around 8 o'clock, we arrived in front of Phil's home. Phil showed up about the same time, and we stopped for a short break. Robert changed his socks and powdered his feet. The break lasted about 30 minutes, until our muscles started to tighten. We got up and moved down the road.

We pulled our boats a couple of more hours, taking a break at the top of each hill. The heat index that day was 110 degrees, making the 350-pound loads nearly unbearable. By late afternoon, my legs were cramping up, head was pounding and my stomach was nauseous.

Eventually, I could go no farther and laid down in my canoe for a 30 minute break.

We pushed on and finally reached the next turn, at a golf course. This road would take us directly into Salem, Missouri, the halfway point.

The heat was taking its toll and we could only pull our canoes about 100 yards before having to stop. We traveled like this all the way to the edge of Salem where we pulled over and took a break underneath a shade tree.

A woman drove up to see what we were up to. The nice lady was a retired police dispatcher. She talked with us for about 30 minutes before continuing on her way. Soon, we were again on the move.

Finally, we portaged into Salem. As we crossed a busy intersection, a man in a big white car stuck his head out the window, and asked, "What in the world are you boys doing?" His name was Dorman, a retired judge. He took a break with us under a shade tree and talked for about 30 minutes. Come to find out, Dorman and his partner (Phil's dad) won the first Current River Canoe Race back in the 60's.

After a little while, he left to get the press. A man with the Salem News showed up about 5 minutes later. He interviewed us and took some pictures, before we moved on.

This time, we were headed in the direction of a motel.

At the motel, I went in to get a room while Robert waited with the gear. A few minutes later, I came out and walked up the street without saying a word. Robert walked in the office to see what the deal was.

The lady at the front desk told him my card didn't work, so Robert put the room on his card and waited for me to return. Half an hour later, I returned and was still extremely furious. I had been calling home for the past two weeks asking those who owed me money to deposit it in my account. They had all failed to do so.

We parked our boats outside the room, went inside and cranked the air conditioner. Robert immediately called his father to thank him for depositing money in his account. I went back outside and talked to our neighbors. I opened the door and tossed Robert a cold drink the neighbors had given me.

Dorman showed up. He had heard about the trouble with my card and said, "I see you boys got a room; you must have worked everything out. I'll see you boys later."

Later that evening, Phil came by to visit. Robert and I told him about the copperhead on the road that morning. Phil informed us that the road was called Copperhead Road for a reason. He introduced us to his father Stephen (Dorman's race partner). He was an oral surgeon with an impressive paddle collection. We went back to the room and shared stories until midnight.

We didn't wake up until 9 o'clock the next morning. The previous day's efforts had left us extremely sore and exhausted, so we decided to rest another day. The motel we were in was booked, so we locked our canoes up at a feed store and walked to the next motel. We rested our sore muscles, caught up on the news, watched TV and absorbed as much air conditioning as possible.

We woke at 3:15 a.m. and walked down to the feed store to retrieve our canoes. We had 17 miles of portaging ahead of us and if all went as planned, we would be on the Current River before noon.

The pace started out fast, walking for over an hour before taking our first break. After re-hydrating with a sports drink, we were off again. Traveling over steep Ozark Mountains and taking breaks at the top of each hill, we were making good time - about 3 miles an hour.

Late morning, we reached the road that would take us to the Current River. A woman on a horse rode up to us and introduced herself as Dr. Pat. She gave us some ice and followed along the last mile to the river. The last half-mile was a steep gravel road winding its way down to the riverbank.

The last 100 feet, we ran to the water's edge. Seeing the clear, cold spring-fed river; we dropped our gear and dove into the water, instantly relieving us from the heat of the day. Just to lie in that river made the torturous portage worth it.

Dr. Pat's father was camped on the river and he handed us a cold drink. We rested just long enough to catch our breath and have a short visit with Dr. Pat and her father. Not wanting to waste away the day, we unloaded our canoes, removed the portage carts and re-packed. We were itching to get back on the water.

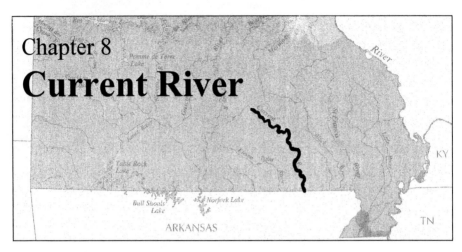

Chapter 8
Current River

July 16 – August 7, 2000

L ife couldn't be better; we were finally going with the flow once again. Not only that, we were on one of the most popular clear water rivers in the country.

Not far from where we put in, we arrived at Welch Spring. The large volume of water flowing from the spring more than doubled the size of the river. It also made the water colder and clearer.

At the same location were the ruins of a health spa specializing in treating lung problems. The stone building was originally built on top of a cave. Years ago, people with breathing problems would lie on stone benches around the cave entrance to breathe the moist, pollen free air. The Missouri Department of Conservation had installed steel bars across the cave entrance to prevent the public from entering and disturbing the endangered Grey Bat that was known to live within.

That afternoon, we made camp about 100 yards below Akers Ferry river access and general store. The operational ferry was still being used for transporting vehicles back and forth across the river. It was also home to one of the largest river outfitters along the Current.

My parents, Larry and Julia Jellison, came to visit for a couple of days. They picked me up, and we went out for supper. I stayed the night with them in a nearby motel, visiting and catching up. We went shopping and they bought several days' worth of food for me to take back to camp.

The next morning, I returned to camp and was not too happy to see Robert had left the lid to my cooler open, melting all the ice. Fortunately, the general store wasn't too far from camp and I was able to get more.

My parents stuck around for a few hours before they said their good-byes and headed back to Tonganoxie, Kansas. It felt good to see them in person instead of just talking on the phone.

We had some friends who were going to join us for a few days. They weren't going to arrive for another five days, so we hung out around camp relaxing, fishing and swimming. Phil came by to check on our progress and to visit.

One morning, before our friends arrived, I woke up early discovering I had been robbed in the night. The masked bandit was a raccoon who took my coffee, water jug, and a cooking pot. He also test tasted a five gallon bucket full of food, that had been divided in zip-lock bags. Each and every bag was torn open and contaminated. I was angry; and to make it worse, Robert was laughing and filming me as I cursed the culprit, which was long gone. All I could picture was a raccoon in a tree filling a pot with water from my jug, making coffee.

The weekend finally arrived and our friends with it. It felt good hanging out around the campfire with familiar faces. The next day, we paddled down river through a traffic jam of canoes. The beautiful summer weather had drawn large crowds to the river looking for a good time. Most of the river users were there for one thing - to party.

Along the way we stopped at Cave Spring, one of the main attractions on the pristine Current River. The large cave entrance allowed canoes to be paddled about 70 feet into the side of an Ozark mountain. At the back of the cave was a large pool of water with the spring emerging from below the surface. This space offered just enough room to turn a canoe around to exit. The water below the

The local folklore was that scuba divers had entered at Devil's Well (located one mile away) and emerged at Cave Spring. Further investigation proved that the underground cave system had been explored by scuba divers, but dye tests were used to actually prove the connection.

60

canoes at that point was over 100 feet deep. Outside the mouth of the cave, daring souls swam the frigid waters flowing out of the ground.

Not far below the cave, we pulled over and made camp. Sitting around the campfire about an hour before sunset, some kids wading down the river, screaming for help, got our attention. With a terrified look on the teenage boys' faces, they told us that one of the two women with them was having a heart attack. Shannon, Silver and I took off running up river as Robert grabbed his canoe and followed us upstream.

Up river about a quarter mile we found a lady in shock, holding a bottle of nitro pills. We left their inner-tubes behind, put her in the canoe and Robert paddled her down to our camp. The girls waiting back at camp helped her out of the canoe and sat her by the campfire to warm her up. Since it was getting dark, we weren't sure what to do. I volunteered to take the women and boys downriver for help. I put the four of them in one of our group's empty canoes and guided them downriver in the fading light of day.

A few miles down river, I saw two guys in a canoe coming upriver looking for the missing people from their group. Happy to be reunited, they asked if I was going to leave them. Looking in their canoe and seeing that they had nothing with them - no gear, no flashlight, not even a life jacket – I told them I couldn't live with myself if I did that.

Now with six people and three canoes to navigate downstream, the obstacles were more difficult to avoid. Several times I had to park my canoe, wade out into the swift current and pull their canoes around difficult obstacles.

After hours of struggle, we came upon a camp with 4x4 vehicles. The friendly campers took the group by pickup down to the river access where the rest of their group was waiting. I paddled on down and arrived at the access before the trucks did.

There was a huge group of people gathered around a park ranger vehicle. Spotting me, several of them ran down to the river's edge and asked, "Have you seen…?" Before they could finish, I cut them off saying, "They're on their way by pick-up." I parked my canoe and walked up to the ranger. I had several questions, including why had no one sent a jet boat up looking for those people.

The ranger informed me they didn't run jet boats at night. I was furious. All day long I had seen tickets being issued for misdemeanor charges; but now that lives were in danger, not a thing was being done. I completed a report, then threw down my sleeping bag and went to sleep.

The next morning I was greeted with a cup of coffee and invited to join the rest of the group for breakfast. The large group was an AA and NA group celebrating their freedom from drugs and alcohol. When I inquired of the distressed woman's condition, I discovered that she was fine. With a full belly, I said goodbye and paddled a couple of miles up river to join my friends as they floated down.

Reunited, we continued downstream, stopping several times to explore caves and overhangs along the way. Robert found an arrowhead in one of the overhangs. The highly detailed artifact was a remnant of the people who inhabited the river valley long ago. Excited about his find, he shared it with the group.

Sunday afternoon had arrived and it was time for our friends to reluctantly return to their lives in Kansas City. We parted ways with our friends at the Pulltite river access.

Before leaving, Robert tried to call John again. We had been trying to contact him for over a week. He was supposed to meet us back at Aker's Ferry to bring us supplies. John wanted us to paddle back upstream to Aker's Ferry where we had already spent five days. Not wanting to back track, we changed the rendezvous point.

The next day, as we were coming down the river, we spotted John's truck crossing the bridge we were passing under. We stood up and waved our hands to get his attention. Not knowing if he saw us or not, we pulled over at the boat ramp next to the bridge.

John and Brian soon found their way down to the river, but without our supplies. John said incase he couldn't find us; he had left all our supplies down river at Two Rivers Canoe Rental. John questioned the speed that we were going. He wondered how we were going so fast and asked me if we were cheating.

His question had not been directed as a joke and I thought to myself about the week we spent waiting to hang out with friends. I changed my demeanor and pointed up to the top of the riverbank and said, "There's a nice flat spot right up there, we could hook it right now if you call me a cheat one more time."

With an alligator smile, John said he was just joking and quickly changed the subject to food and beer. He pointed out that he had a full cooler and we needed to find a campsite so he could grill us all steaks.

A few hundred yards down river at Round Spring, we met up with John and made camp. John set up his stove and informed everyone that he didn't have the setup to cook steaks, so he boiled some hotdogs instead. It didn't really matter because sleep was the only thing we were thinking about.

After two more days of paddling, we arrived at Two Rivers Canoe Outfitters at the confluence of the Current and Jack's Fork Rivers and picked up our buckets of supplies that John left. About the time we were ready to leave, a reporter from the Current Wave newspaper showed up and interviewed us. After posing for several pictures, we said our goodbye's to the great people at Two Rivers Canoe Rental and continued our journey.

© Photo courtesy of Julia Jellison

The next day we arrived at Big Spring, where we waited a few days for some of Robert's family to arrive. Robert went into town with his brother, Kenny, and family. I stayed behind to watch the gear. For the next day and a half, I watched drunken tubers and paddlers parade by. It was like watching Mardi Gras on water. After Robert's visit with his family, we explored the site where Big Spring emerges.

The sight was breathtaking. The spring boiled clear cold water in the form of a Class III rapid from a hole at the base of a bluff. The water flowed about a thousand feet before joining the Current River. With an average flow of 277 million gallons of water a day, it was ranked as the country's largest spring (and one of the world's largest).

Below Big Spring, the river was much wider and heavily used by motor boats. We paddled 30 more miles through the Mark Twain National Forest before reaching the town of Doniphan. We were at the end of the designated Ozark National Scenic Waterway and this was our last opportunity, in Missouri, to re-supply.

The next day we passed over the Arkansas state line headed towards the Black River.

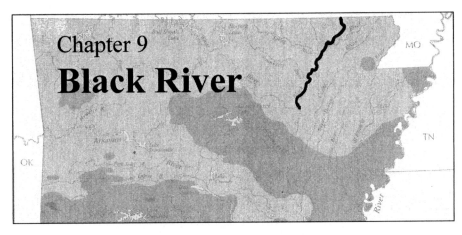

Chapter 9
Black River

August 7 – 14, 2000

The terrain changed before our eyes as we left the Ozark Hills behind and entered the Arkansas Delta region. The land was flat with nothing but rice fields all around. Arkansas was the #1 rice producing state in the nation, and with all the standing water, there were mosquitoes - lots of mosquitoes. The mosquitoes were so thick bug repellant did not even begin to provide protection. The sound of large diesel powered pumps were heard constantly pumping water into the rice fields.

Large swarms of dragonflies hovered as far as the eye could see. The banks of the river were covered with sand fleas so thick that when walking over them, it appeared as though the sand moved with us. At night, they sounded like popcorn as they bounced off the tents. Each morning we had several green frogs hitching a ride in the es. The water was murky and alive with fish rolling on the surface.

It was miserably hot, with daily temperatures reaching 100 degrees or higher before figuring in the heat index. On top of that, it was very humid.

We stopped at Pocahontas, Arkansas, for last minute supplies before moving on. Later that evening, two fishermen stopped by our camp and offered us a cold beer. One of them introduced himself as Gomer Pile. They were the only other people we saw on the river, mainly because of the mosquitoes. I offered them bug repellant, but they waved it off explaining, "We're drinking it."

The fishermen continued on upstream to set out catfish lines and came back to camp a little after dark. They promised to bring back McDonald's breakfast in the morning, "right at sunrise". Robert and I laughed thinking, surely they were joking. We had looked at the map, and there wasn't a town for miles. As the fishermen motored down river, a large cloud of mosquitoes followed their spotlight.

Right at sunrise, we heard an outboard motor coming up river. The fishermen pulled up and, as promised, handed over a bag full of slowly cooling McDonald's breakfast, with a couple of Cokes. The fishermen were a little hung over from drinking so much "mosquito repellant."

We stopped at the Old Davidsonville Museum and Powhattan Courthouse State Park. At the courthouse, we met Eleanor, a member of a historical group who helped to revive various sites in the area.

They had restored the old courthouse, jail, a log home, as well as, other American historic sites in the area.

Many years ago, the town flourished from the mussel industry. Fresh water pearls were harvested from the mussels. The empty shells went into warehouses where they were used to make buttons. Every part was used, even the remnants of the shells were ground up and used for hog feed. Millions of shells were harvested; pictures of barges piled up with shells could be seen on the walls of the old courthouse. As the demand for these buttons declined, so did the town. This stop along the journey gave us an interesting view of American history that was new to us.

A good day's travel downstream, we met Jeff and Tim who were installing a new pump in a well-house next to an old river cabin. They were converting the property into a hunt camp - called 7-Mile Loop. They were headed back into town for the night, but told us we could use the cabin. It had a large screened in porch, perfect for the hot

Arkansas summer nights. Jeff and Tim had left us some cold beers and a bottle of moonshine. We had a good nights sleep after a few cold beers chased with a snort of moonshine.

The next day, we helped Jeff and Tim finish wiring the well. We talked a while and were invited to stay another night. I was the first to take a shower with the camps new well. We repeated the previous night's nightcap, watching shooting stars and listening to the mosquitoes hum on the opposite side of the screened in porch.

Just down river, we found a wave runner that was half submerged in a root wad. After further investigation, we found a fist size hole in the bow of the vessel. Robert and I pulled the wave runner out of the water and patched the hole with duct tape. It almost started when we tried the key, which was amazing because it had obviously been there a long time. We took turns towing it down river and gave it to the first person we saw. At least it no longer trashed up the river.

Chapter 10
White River

August 14 – 30, 2000

In the delta it was wise to stop before sunset and set up camp. The mosquitoes attacked us so badly at sunset that stepping out of the tent, even if only for a moment, we would find ourselves covered with hundreds of them. Determined to get to the White River before setting up camp, we arrived shortly after dark and were attacked by thousands of the little bloodsuckers.

The next morning we arrived at Jacksonport State Park. Renovation was underway on an old paddleboat there. Even though it was closed to the public, we were given permission to look around. After exploring the paddleboat, we went to the visitors' center in town and toured the Confederate Soldiers' memorial. The whole town was being renovated from tornadoes that had destroyed the area a year prior. However, very little damage was still visible.

A care package was on the way to the post office in Newport, five miles downriver, but wouldn't arrive for three days. So, we made camp at the state park in Jacksonport where the local folks were friendly and anxious to help-out. One morning, walking up to the bathhouse, I met a writer for the Jackson County Paper. I told him about our expedition, and the writer wanted to meet up with us for an interview.

Kelly, the reporter, returned the next morning, just before sunrise. I went with him into town to get some coffee and check my e-mail. Kelly and I got back around noon and he talked with both of us for over an hour. The next day, he took Robert into town to check his e-mail.

On the last morning in Jacksonport, Kelly came by our campsite to say goodbye and told us to stop a little ways further down at his friend's trailer. After a 30-minute paddle, we arrived and had breakfast. Kelly gave Robert a ride to the Newport post office to pick up his care packages, while I stayed behind with the gear. After going through the packages, Robert and I loaded up our canoes and continued on, paddling 25 miles that day.

The White River passed through the White River National Wildlife Reserve. Just below the locks connecting to Marasak Lake, we spotted a small black bear with a radio collar around its neck. We paddled to within 20 feet of the bear. It seemed to have no fear of humans as we took a few photographs and made camp just down river.

The next morning, we maneuvered through two locks paddling against 30 mph winds onto Marasak Lake. The lake connected the Arkansas River with the White River for barge traffic. The Arkansas Post Museum was located on the lake. We paddled to the Post to pickup my mail.

The package had not arrived, so to beat the heat, we took advantage of the museum's air conditioning. The historian working there was very educational and hospitable. Spain, France and then the United States had occupied the historically significant army post. It was also the site of one of the most important Civil War victories of the North. Outside the museum an alligator lay motionless below the surface of the water as we walked back to our canoes. It was the first, of many, we would see on the journey.

It was late afternoon and we needed to get moving to find a place to camp. With both hands full, I stepped down on the bow of my canoe, trying to avoid the swamp mud. I looked down and within inches from my sandaled foot was a cottonmouth coiled up ready to strike. I jumped back on the shore one legged, just in time.

The snake then slithered down under the gear hiding in my canoe. We started carefully removing gear, but it kept moving further towards the back of the canoe. Finally, we had the serpent cornered in the back of the canoe. We tried fishing it out of the boat with a paddle, but it refused. Coiled up, it bit and swallowed one of the hitchhiking green frogs. Satisfied, it then slithered over the edge and swam away. From then on, all frogs were jettisoned by Jellison.

The sun was setting fast and the mosquitoes were beginning to feed. The only decent camp spot was across the lake. Robert and I dug hard to reach the distant bank arriving after dark. We quickly set up our tents in the dark and took refuge from the bugs.

Nearly asleep, a man pulled up in a pickup and told us we were not allowed to camp there. We told him we had paddled there from Kansas City and didn't want to move in the bug swarms. The mosquitoes were taking this opportunity to feed on the man. Understanding our predicament, he gave us permission and drove away.

The next day, we returned to the Arkansas Post to find my mail had arrived. We paddled back through the locks and down the White River. We saw a huge mama bear and two cubs that were feeding on dead fish left behind by commercial fisherman. After photographing them, we paddled a short distance arriving at the mouth of the White River.

Chapter 11
Mississippi River – part two

August 30 –
September 13, 2000

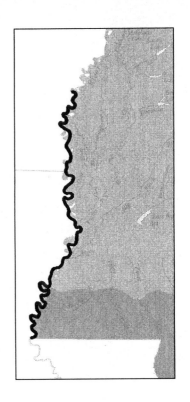

The mouth of the White River opened up wide dumping us out onto the muddy Mississippi River. The wide channeled river was lined with beautiful sandbars. Large thunderstorms passed through and gave the most impressive lightning shows we had ever seen. As scary as the storms were, it brought temporary relief to the extreme heat.

We landed near Rosedale, Mississippi, at a rock quarry. A man named Condor gave us a ride to town to get supplies.

Continuing on down river, the heat had returned. To get relief and still make progress, we spent a lot of time swimming along side the canoes as we drifted down the middle of the Mississippi River. Some people told us we were crazy for swimming with the alligators, but it felt better than just frying out in the sun. Whenever a barge would come along, we would climb back in our canoes and paddle out of harms way.

Arriving at Greenville, Mississippi, we were greeted by a man at the Greenville Yacht Club. After hearing our story, he told us, "Yankees! Park your boats and come inside for a cold drink."

The Pirates of the Mississippi, a boat club, were using the yacht club for a big rally. Robert and I were invited to stay for the festivities. Robert was meeting an old flame there, so we took them up on their invitation.

We stayed at a local motel near the water. After cleaning up, I headed to the party. On my way from the motel, a limousine pulled up next to me and asked if I was a "pirate". I told him no, but that's where I was headed. The guy said to hop in and I arrived to the party in style, going for my first limo ride. We left Greenville fully loaded with supplies.

The Mississippi River was channeled via levees and wing dams, but still offered one of a kind beauty. The banks were lined with trees where wildlife could be seen coming out for a drink of water. Occasionally we spotted alligators swimming in the muddy river. With the powerful current pushing us downstream, it was not hard to achieve 40 miles in a day.

At a public boat ramp in Natchez, Mississippi, we saw the most unusual catamaran. It was made of two canoes, fully rigged with sail and mast; and it was tie-dyed and covered with peace signs. We walked up the steep ramp and spotted a neat little pub - called Under the Hill.

Under the Hill was built in the 1800's, and still had a very rustic look and feel. The upstairs had several rooms for rent at a reasonable price. The entire front of the building was designed so that large doors could swing open creating an open-air space with a spectacular view overlooking the Mississippi River. It was the coolest river front pub we had ever seen. After a couple of cold drinks, we continued on our way.

Down river we passed huge sandbars, some several acres in size. Barges that were much larger than those found on the Missouri River, kicked up massive wakes as they passed by us. Some of the push boat pilots would toot their horns, while the deck hands sometimes waved friendly. After the upstream barges would pass, we paddled out behind them to play in the 4-6 foot standing waves. What a rush! We called this "riding the dragon" because it felt like a massive serpent was trying to throw us off its back.

Just above Baton Rouge we came to the Atchafalaya cut. Southbound Mississippi River traffic that was headed westward used this man-made canal to connect to the Atchafalaya River. Pulling up to the lock, the operator in the tower above could not see our two canoes. I climbed the hillside and knocked on the control booth door. The man inside was shocked when I told him that there were two canoes waiting to be locked thru. Usually larger boats were the only traffic using the lock and he simply did not see us.

As we locked through the canal, we saw thousands of love bugs, an alligator, dozens of egrets and two coyotes. We made camp on the Atchafalaya side of the lock and discovered a plague that has taken over a lot of the South - fire ants. The pests were able to find and penetrate the tinniest hole in a tent. They got their name from the pain inflicted from their bites. When bitten, it felt as though that part of the body was on fire. An army of the tiny pests tormented us throughout the night. After little sleep, we paddled out of the canal into the wide and deep Atchafalaya River.

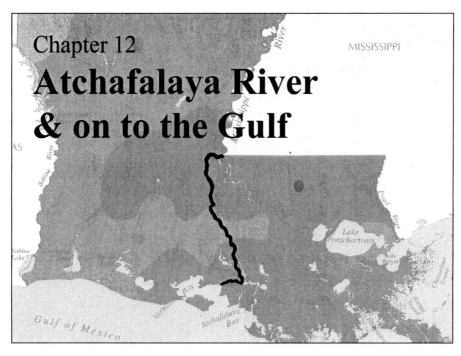

Chapter 12
Atchafalaya River & on to the Gulf

September 14 – October 10, 2000

Several people had warned us of the dangerous conditions found on the Atchafalaya River—under currents, large debris—but the river seemed mostly harmless as we continued south toward the Gulf of Mexico.

At Simsport, Louisiana, a high bridge crossed the river. Atop that bridge was a wiry man with a paint pot and a brush painting the bridge. About a hundred feet up he yelled down, "Where you put in?"

"Kansas City," we answered.

"You crazy!" he replied in a deep Cajun accent.

We answered, "You're the one who's crazy, up there with no safety equipment!"

He then yelled to his ground man, "You hear that? They came all the way from Kansas City and are calling me crazy!" He stood there like a rooster high on his perch as Robert and I waved and paddled on.

By mid-afternoon we were getting low on drinking water. We spotted a building that looked like some kind of business and pulled up to the muddy riverbank below. Two men appeared at the top of the bank, so we asked if we could fill our water jugs, and the older of the two said, "Come on."

We waded through knee deep mud with our empty jugs to dry ground and introduced ourselves. The older man introduced himself as Alex, and after we rinsed off the mud, he invited us inside.

To our surprise, the plain looking building was a club with a bar, dance floor, stage, gambling machines and the loudest jukebox ever. After talking a while, Alex grabbed a set of keys and said, "Come with me."

Alex insisted that we stay a while and led us to a two-bedroom cabin telling us we could stay as long as we wanted. "Get cleaned up, 'cause I've got some girls that are go'na dance your legs off!" he said as he handed us another cold drink. With an offer like that, we couldn't refuse.

In Melville, Louisiana, at Alex's Place, no one went home hungry. The busy bar maid, as well as serving drinks, cooked a fine Cajun meal. It was more than enough for everyone at the club, and to our surprise everyone ate for free. After telling our story dozens of times, and partying well into the night, we both slept comfortably in real beds.

The next morning, Alex greeted us bearing food and drink. He asked if we would like to make some money fixing up the outside of the place. Since we were always in need of more money for the expedition, we took him up on the offer. Alex wouldn't let us spend a dime. He provided all our meals, drinks, and snacks.

After working and partying all weekend, we loaded up and took a road trip over to Slidell, Louisiana. Alex had a large "camp" bordering the Pearl River National Wildlife Refuge. Following our tour of the several hundred acre hunt camp, we loaded up a trailer full of building material and headed back to Melville.

We spent the rest of the week building a huge patio over looking the river. We also constructed several gazeboes for Alex's campground behind the club and seats for his pier that extended out over the river's edge, adjacent to the club.

Even though we were itching to make miles, Alex talked us into staying another weekend. The town was having a Fair and a Catfish

Tournament on Saturday. It was Thursday, so we continued working around the place to pass the time. Robert worked on his video camera, which was now dead.

That night, Robert met a good-looking woman in her "daisy dukes". After talking to her for a couple of hours, the guy next to her says, "Honey, let's go home."

Her husband had been there, listening to them flirt the entire time! Before leaving, she told Robert, "I should have married you." Robert and I laughed off the incident, until later when the husband returned with his head wrapped up in bandages.

Someone at the bar asked, "What happened?"

The man responded, "She stabbed me with a screwdriver! I knew she was crazy, but didn't know how crazy." He had a beer and left to go bail her out!

Friday, I went to the fair with some of the money I made working for Alex. I enjoyed some great Cajun food and music. That night, back at the club, we danced with some of the local girls until two in the morning.

The day of the big catfish tournament, Robert and I woke up hung over. We climbed into our canoes and paddled up river to try our luck. The fishing was slow, so I took a nap on the river bank until being suddenly awakened by a ferocious little dog that insisted I leave.

I screamed, "Go on, get!" but the wild little dog kept coming at me. I jumped up and had to shoo it away with my paddle as the dog continued its attack. Eventually, it got the message and trotted off down river.

At the same time elsewhere, Robert was taking a nap next to some homemade catfish bait when he was awakened covered with fire ants. His first reaction was to jump in the river, but doing so only made things worse. This triggered the army of fire ants to simultaneously attack. He arrived back at camp covered with bites and only a goo fish, commonly known as a black drum, to show for the day's efforts.

At the fish weigh-in, the same little dog that tried to attack me came back upriver along the bank. I asked who the dog belonged to, and a couple of people responded, "He's his own."

I told them of my run in with the dog and everybody there started laughing. One man with a thick Cajun accent said, "You ain't the first. That his river in his mind."

Come to find out, the heathen dog had been patrolling the riverbank and running people off for some time. Pretty amazing animal since dogs are considered a delicacy to alligators, which attack and eat them regularly in the area.

That night we cleaned up and went into the club. The bartender's son, an extremely large man, beat Robert in an arm wrestling match. The guy then challenged me. After I beat him three times in a row, the big man was furious. He yelled, "How can a scrawny little runt like you be so strong?" He went on to tell me how he had been an all state lineman for his high school football team before stomping off.

Later, a girl dared me to get up and sing karaoke. I was the first to sing that night and had everybody dancing. I danced with the same girl for a couple of songs before being approached by the large lineman. Pointing his finger in my face, he physically threatened me with violence for dancing with his girl. Sitting in a chair, looking up at the monster, I knew the large man had the advantage and could probably have crushed me into the very chair I was sitting in. I looked into the bully's eyes and bluffed, "No your not, you can't."

Furious, the guy stormed over to Robert and told him, "You better get your friend away from her!"

Robert barely acknowledged him, and said, "May the best man win."

The girl denied having any relationship with the large man. However, the guy tried several times to cut in on us, out on the dance floor. After several denials from the lady, he finally got the hint and left the establishment.

Late in the evening there was an anonymous request for me to sing again. I accepted the challenge and near the end of the song a woman from the crowd got on stage and finished the song with me.

Before she left the stage, she planted a big kiss on me and scampered away, with her angry husband staring me down.

Robert walked up to me and said, "Stop doing that. These girls are going to get us killed!"

I apologized to the woman's husband, but he didn't even spare me a glance. I then said goodbye to the girl I had danced with most of the evening, and returned to the cabin.

When I walked in, Robert was already there. Robert said, "I got a bad feeling. There's a lot of pissed off men around here tonight."

Just before light began to show from the eastern skies, I awoke to a barley audible tapping noise followed by Robert whispering my name. Immediately I stood up and opened the door to my room. I found Robert lying on the floor in the prone position with his rifle pointed at the front door. He whispered to me that somebody was trying to break in. With my pistol in hand, I whispered, "You ready?"

Robert nodded, yes and I kicked the front door open. Quickly stepping out into the darkness, I yelled, "You want in so bad, well here I am!" I drew down left as Robert swept right, searching for our target. We heard footsteps rapidly moving away into the woods behind the cabin, before they came to a stop.

Robert and I knew better than to follow them into the woods with it still being dark. We searched around the cabin to make sure the perimeter was clear, keeping an ear open to the woods, listening for movement.

With the area secure, I yelled, "It's almost light and you're going to die!"

A few moments later, the sound of running started again. We then heard a horse nay, followed by a fast paced gallop, moving away from our location.

Not long after sunrise, Alex showed up and saw we were packing up to leave. We weren't sticking around to have ourselves turned into gator-bait. Alex had treated us so well; it was a shame to have to leave on that note. Alex, being the generous man that he was, gave us an additional $200 in travel money along with our pay. Except for the last little incident, Melville had been great.

As we paddled away, our guns were easily accessible, laying out in plain view. We dug hard with our paddles to make miles, constantly scanning the bank for an ambush. It felt good to be moving again, even if we were a little on edge. The river was turning to swamp with Cypress trees covered in Spanish moss in constant view.

Evening was fast approaching and we had not seen a decent place to camp for hours. The only dry land in sight was covered with alligator tracks and slides. It was getting dark and the mosquitoes were unbearable. We finally found a place to camp and quickly got into our tents.

Robert was listening to his radio when I heard something that sounded huge running towards camp, knocking down grass, brush, and anything in its path. I screamed, "We got movement!" as I bailed out of my tent, gun and flashlight in hand, ready to shoot. The movement stopped 15 feet away from our tents in tall marsh grass. With my finger on the trigger, I sat motionless waiting for any movement.

Several minutes passed when Robert said, "There's an armadillo looking in my tent and it looks scared."

I responded, "Whatever it was, sure as heck wasn't that little thing."

The mosquitoes were so thick I was breathing them in. As I started to get back into my tent, Robert said, "If I was a gator, you would probably look like a hotdog in that tiny little tent."

I slept in Robert's tent that night, which was much bigger and had a full 360° view.

The next morning we looked around and found the tracks of an alligator that had to have been 10 feet long. It seems we had camped in its yard.

The next night I woke to Robert cursing out into the darkness. The river had risen considerably and took off with Robert's canoe that he had forgotten to tie down. Unable to find his canoe in the dark, we used mine for the search; but were unsuccessful.

The next morning we woke up at first light to fog so thick we couldn't see the river; much less Robert's missing canoe. Through the fog we heard a barge coming upstream. All we could picture was Robert's canoe being chewed up by the large propellers.

A couple of hours later the fog lifted and with all Robert's gear loaded up in my canoe, we moved on. Unable to fit in the boat, Robert walked through the swamp along the river. Several alligators dove into the river only a few feet ahead of him as he tried to keep up with me.

A few miles downstream Robert shot off his gun three times indicating that he saw his canoe. I rounded the bend of the river to see Robert's canoe up on the bank. It looked as though somebody had drug it up out of the river, but there were no footprints. Robert thanked God that we were able to find his canoe. I towed the canoe across the river to Robert where we transferred his gear and moved on.

We traveled for several days without seeing a soul and then came upon a boat tied up along the shore. Two men immerged from the swamp as Robert and I paddled up. They introduced themselves as Wild Man and Viking. They told us of a cut through the swamp that would get us over to the Bayou Teche and into the Intra-Coastal Waterway.

We tied up our canoes and hopped into their boat to scout out the route. Weaving through the swamp for about an hour, we found the route we needed to take. Heading back to the canoes, we saw several wild hogs feeding along the river. Viking grabbed Robert's gun to take a shot at them but was surprised to find that the gun was unloaded.

Back in the canoes, we started searching for a place to camp. We cleared off some river cane from the only dry land we had seen for a while in order to make camp. Listening to the symphony of frogs, crickets and mosquitoes echoing across the swamp late into the night, I finally got some sleep.

The next morning we paddled down river through thick fog. Moving slowly along the bank, I noticed a huge eight-foot alligator swimming along side. It was so close, I could have reached down and touched it. Knowing how an alligator could easily flip a boat, I stopped paddling until it cleared the front of my canoe.

As the fog lifted, the beauty of the swamp was revealed. Large cypress trees draped with Spanish moss covered the landscape. Now closer than ever to the Gulf of Mexico, the river was wide open resembling a lake.

Following directions from Wild Man and Viking, we portaged over a levee and paddled down a small bayou that poured into the famous Bayou Teche. Our route would lead us west toward the Baldwin Spillway that would take us due south into the Intra-Coastal Waterway.

The Bayou Teche had been used since long before Louisiana became a state, back to a time when pirates sailed the seas. The bayou was lined with homes; most of which had a water vessel parked along the water's edge - from kayaks to float planes. The homes ranged in size from one room shacks to the Governor's Mansion.

We arrived in Franklin and stopped at the sheriff's office to find a place to store our canoes while we went into town to do some shopping. The sheriff allowed us to leave the canoes inside the courthouse parking garage. The sign above the stall stated, "Prisoner Parking Only."

We spent the night in a motel thanks to the money we made working for Alex Dugas. We were ready for an opportunity to get cleaned up and out of the bugs because the next several hundred miles would be in brackish water.

The next morning we thanked the sheriff and portaged 50 yards back to the Bayou Teche. The canal was very narrow with lily pads covering most of it. Several miles down, a small private barge was headed right toward us. The canal was so narrow, we had no choice but to head for shore. Before getting there the barge stole all the water, leaving us on dry land. As soon as the barge passed, a wall of water returned like a miniature tsunami, threatening to capsize our boats. The barge lost control and smashed into shore. After a few minutes of maneuvering, the captain was able to free himself and continue on.

Reaching the Baldwin Spillway, the terrain turned to marsh with only a small patch of dry land here and there. As we paddled down the man-made canal, we saw water birds fishing along the shore. Some dove from the air into the water reemerging with lunch. As far as we could see, were the open waters of the Gulf of Mexico!

Out of nowhere a large commercial barge crossed our path, indicating we had finally arrived at the Intra-Coastal Waterway. This fulfilled our childhood dreams of traveling the rivers from home to the Gulf of Mexico. We had come so far, yet the journey had only begun.

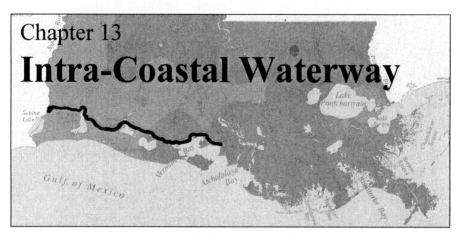

Chapter 13
Intra-Coastal Waterway

October 10 – 27, 2000

Arriving at the intra-coastal waterway, we turned west through the barge-infested swamp. Alligators were all over the place, most not having any fear. Most evenings in the swamp ended with an amazing sunset. Commercial fishermen frequently stopped to give us fish and wished us good luck as they departed. Even though a lot of people were friendly, some were bitter and mean. In Intra-Costal City the dock man cursed us for asking where a grocery store could be found.

Near Grand Lake we met a man in a small restaurant who invited us to stay and get cleaned up at his place. He told us to call him when we were near his home and he would help us out. We called the phone number he gave us, but another man named Doug, answered the phone. After hearing our story, he drove down from his camp and picked us up at the water with a flatbed trailer.

THE INTRA-COASTAL WATERWAY was dug several decades ago to insure the safe passage of watercraft along the coast. It does this utilizing a land barrier between the boats and the brutal wind and water found on the open seas. There are several sections that are open to the Gulf. Some of the bays leave you unprotected for miles of open seas.

Doug's Hunt Camp was the second largest waterfowl hunting camp in Louisiana. Robert and I dropped off our gear and Doug and his wife took us out for supper. On the way home, Doug dropped us off at the house of the man we had originally met.

The man turned out to be the biggest jerk we had met thus far on the journey. The more he drank, the more of a jerk he became. He made comments like, "You have a zero-percent-chance of making it to the Pacific." And, "I'll buy you bus tickets to go home now."

Robert and I wanted to leave, but were in a dilemma; stay there and be insulted, or walk 10 miles at night in swarms of mosquitoes. The guy's wife was silent with nothing but shame on her face. Finally he drove us back to camp. Normally we wouldn't ride with a drunk driver, but it was a chance we were willing to take.

Doug was the complete opposite. He was a very generous and kind man. He insisted we stay and rest awhile, and gave us the keys to one of the cabins on the retreat. The cabin was more than relaxing with satellite TV, beds and all the comforts of home. We took a well-needed break.

Salt water was taking its toll on our gear and bank accounts. Everything metal was corroded with rust and some of it so bad it had to be thrown away. Doug gave us permission to rummage through the lost and found boxes, which helped out a lot. He then threw us the keys to his new pick-up to go to town and buy the rest of our replacement gear.

Outfitted with gear and food we rested for several days, barely moving from the couch. My elbow needed the rest. I had been in severe pain for days due to an inflamed tendon caused by endless repetitive motion.

After a well needed rest, our sunburns, windburns and other ailments were mostly healed. Anxious to be on the water again, we headed out.

Leaving the protection of the Intra-Coastal Waterway, we paddled across Calcasieu Lake. Everything seemed surreal as thousands of birds could be seen in every direction. Channel markers were white

94

from birds nesting and roosting on them. Sea gulls hovered above looking for handouts.

Reality set in when strong winds began to blow. We battled against high seas and strong gusts of winds for a couple of hours before reaching the safety of the Intra-Coastal Waterway again.

For weeks we had been warned that the Sabine River delta was known for the worst mosquito problems of the Gulf Coast. When we arrived there, we discovered that all the rumors were true. Ship crossing signs posted along the canal were the least of our concerns. Mosquitoes were the problem and there were millions of them. It was the middle of the day with 30-mph winds, and the bugs were so thick we couldn't help but breathe them in.

Crossing the Sabine into Texas, we beached our canoes as a middle-aged man approached us. It was surprising to see anyone, considering the remoteness of the area. He insisted that we move on stating that we were on private property.

We asked how he got back in there and if there was a town nearby. He informed us that Orange, Texas, was not far. Then he asked the magic question, "Where did you put in?"

Upon our response, he thought we were joking, but after looking us over he realized the truth of our words.

His attitude completely changed and he asked what we wanted from town. Drinking water was all we needed and he told us to make camp on the oil pier. "There's less mosquitoes over the water." he said as he drove off and saying he would be right back.

We set up camp on the pier, but the mosquitoes were still overwhelming and made life miserable. When he returned, he had a reporter from the Orange, Texas, city paper with him. It was one of the shortest interviews due to the plague of mosquitoes. They took pictures and departed.

Even though it seemed impossible, the camping only got worse as we continued into Texas.

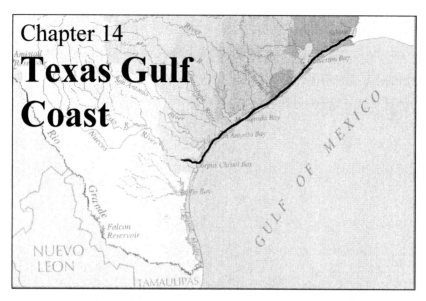

Chapter 14
Texas Gulf Coast

October 27 – December 5, 2000

The intra-coastal waterway along the Texas Gulf Coast was mostly fields of marsh grass. Several nights the only dry place to camp was on top of tree roots. We would set up our tents and then place them on top of a root system. My tent provided protection from the bugs. However, Robert's tent zipper had failed due to corrosion and he suffered miserably for a couple of weeks. We were completely exhausted because sleeping was so uncomfortable and nearly impossible.

Larger boats were present in addition to the normal barge traffic. One boat in particular was what we called, "The canoe killer." We could hear it coming as far as we could see it. The vessel was a large flat bed boat that re-supplied the oil fields in the Gulf of Mexico. When passing, not only did it steal the water from under us, it sent a three foot barrel wave in both directions from its bow to the bank. The captains of these boats would approach at a high speed and then at the last second, slow to an idol and get a good laugh at our expense.

The closest call we had with commercial traffic was with a barge. The Intra-Coastal Waterway has a main channel, but along the outside of the channel was a wide, very shallow flat. As barges passed, the water over the shallow flat was pulled away leaving small boats dry-docked waiting for the barge to pass. After passing, the water returned in a sudden rush.

As this particular barge was headed for us, we moved out of the way into the shallow water to wait for it to pass - as usual. As the distance between the barge and the canoes decreased, for some unknown reason it turned, until it was pointed straight at us. At the last minute the captain turned the wheel causing the water to push a three-foot high barrel of water toward us instead of pulling the water away. Only a few feet away from the barge and dangerously close to it's propellers that were kicking up mud, I hit the wave and the canoe became airborne. Somehow I stayed in the boat and landed upright with little water in the canoe. I turned around to watch Robert finishing a repeat of what had just happened to me.

We escaped death only by inches. Robert and I both gave them the finger and called them every name in the book. The whole incident seemed intentional and uncalled for.

Crossing Galveston Bay proved to be another challenge. Not only did we have to battle wind, waves and barge traffic, but ships were everywhere. The water began to clear as we paddled out in the bay. Several porpoise swam around us, some within five feet of the canoes.

The further we got from shore, the larger the waves grew. It was like we were in a large wash-tub, battling five-foot waves. After several miles of rough water we landed on Galveston Island. We toured an old war submarine and ship that were part of a military museum.

Moving on we made camp near Rollover Pass. The island acquired its name during Prohibition when barrels of whiskey were rolled over the island. From the sheltered waters on the other side smaller boats would then haul the merchandise inland using small tributaries.

The next day we went into town and some local media showed up to cover our story. The locals were very "Texas-friendly" and hospitable.

While there I feared I would have to hitchhike home. I hadn't had a proper meal in weeks and was completely broke. Even after I made several calls to people that owed me money, none of the funds I needed were being deposited into my account.

I stopped at an ATM to check my balance and discovered $1200 in the account. I danced a jig right there with several people looking on, and hollered to Robert, "I'm rich, I'm rich!" People looked at me like I was crazy. The last person I expected to pay finally came through. It was a huge relief. We stopped at a local restaurant and ate several meals at one sitting.

Paddling southwest through Christmas Bay, the sky grew dark and the wind began to blow. We made camp on a small peninsula where the ground was made entirely of seashells, making it impossible to secure our tents to the ground. Seventy mile-per-hour winds ripped through the area with rain so hard it blew right through the tents. Large waves crashed on shore stopping only a few feet away. Our canoes filled with water from the incoming waves and tidal waters before we could drag them to higher ground. With nothing to secure them to, we left the water in the canoes to keep them from blowing away.

For three days and nights the storm blew. We were marooned, stuck in our tents. Everything we owned was soaking wet. The temperature stayed in the 40's leaving us cold, wet, and shivering the entire time.

Day three, looking out of our tents, a coyote stood only 10 feet away looking at us. We told it, "We aren't dead yet!" and it scurried away. Finally the sky cleared and in minutes our gear was loaded and we left the miserable camp.

Not far down the coast, we arrived at San Luis Pass Pier, a Texas fishing hot spot. We met Bob, the owner, and made camp on the beach next to the pier, since it was free. After the storm we needed to dry gear and make repairs to my canoe.

My canoe had been falling apart since the Meramec River, but now it was nearly useless. Oyster reefs had cut holes through the canoe where delaminating had taken place, not to mention several other factory defects. I had been sold a lemon. Contacting the manufacturer, they seemed willing to help. All I needed to do was take the canoe to the nearest representative and get a new one. So, I hitched a ride up to Houston R.E.I. The canoe specialist there contacted a representative of the canoe manufacturer, clearly stating the problems were a result of manufacture defects. The materials used in the trim were defective and the hull was almost completely delaminated. Robert's canoe was older and still in good shape.

The representative on the phone told me they would replace the canoe for $500 and that it would take two weeks for delivery. This completely contradicted what I was told just hours earlier, leaving me silent and confused. The representative responded, "You don't sound very happy."

"Why should I be happy about being screwed over?" I snapped back. All that went through my head was a mental picture of my paperwork stating the canoe had a three-year warranty on the hull.

He responded, "I'm sorry you feel this way, but you're excessively abusing the boat."

I told him how Robert's canoe was a year old before we left and it appeared nearly new after traveling side by side with me. In addition, Robert abused his canoe more, sometimes dragging it dozens of yards over rough terrain fully loaded; where as, I unloaded and carried everything on my back.

The company representative responded in a monotone voice, "That's the best offer we can give you."

Without wasting any more time, I handed the phone back over to the R.E.I. employee. With a puzzled look, the guy hung up the phone. He then gave me a new Kevlar skid plate kit for no charge and apologized. The guy then simply stated, "You'd think for what you're doing they would give you as many canoes as you needed."

I told him how we had contacted the company prior to the trip and how they had no interest in helping out. The people at R.E.I. Houston were kind and helpful, but leaving there, I knew time and money had been wasted on trying to replace my canoe.

Back at camp, I told Robert what had happened and he was even madder than me. Trying to be optimistic, I began repairs. In between coats there was dry time, before applying additional coats. During that time I did some fishing, catching several large gaff top fish and stingray off the pier. After extensive patch work on the canoe, it was again seaworthy, and we were able to continue on with the expedition.

Down the coast, my weather radio gave us bad news that another large storm was headed our way. We got a room at Linda's Bait

Camp in Sergeant, Texas. Linda's husband, a shrimp boat captain for many years, was locally known for being the toughest man around. By the looks of him, Robert and I had no reason to doubt his credibility. We told him about our plan to cross Matagorda Bay and he looked at us like we were plain stupid. He then told us we could make it if the seas were calm. He went on to tell horror stories of how boats much larger than ours were commonly lost attempting to cross. Hearing this dampened our enthusiasm, but we were still undaunted.

Three days of brutal weather later, we packed our canoes to leave. Before departing, Linda reimbursed a night's stay in cash and wished us good luck.

Twenty-two miles later, after passing through the Colorado River locks, we were exhausted and made camp. A huge feral pig of 300 pounds walked up to the edge of camp. We grabbed our guns, not wanting to miss a chance to get fresh meat. Before we could get a shot off, the pig fled never to be seen again.

That night we had picked a poor place to camp. The barges locking through had no choice but to moor near us, making it difficult to sleep with their idling diesel engines turning all night. One of the moored barges thought it would be funny to spotlight our camp with their powerful airplane lights. As time passed, we got more and more aggravated. We stepped out of our tents and yelled at the men aboard, followed by an invitation to come ashore and settle it once and for all. The men onboard erupted with drunken laughter, and there were no takers on the invitation.

More time passed and we actually thought about shooting the lights out, but feared killing someone over a childish prank. Over an hour had passed with their spotlight and verbal taunts. We had taken more than anyone should have to take and simultaneously, got out of our tents with guns in hand. The spotlight turned off.

With little sleep the night before, we reached a long line of mooring buoys marking the edge of Matagorda Bay. There was nothing but high seas as far as the eye could see and not a speck of land visible on the horizon. Through binoculars we watched large

boats in the distance disappear behind waves to reemerge in-between the crests. To paddle out into the bay would be suicide. We made camp near the buoys and waited where many before us had done in the past. We spent the afternoon hiking around camp and found several old bottles dating back to the 50's and 60's. It was a nice distraction from what lie ahead.

Before sunrise, on November 22, 2000, we were packed and on our way. My weather radio warned of a small watercraft advisory for the bay. I turned it off and stowed it away. Today was the day, do or die. The wind began to pick up. Large swells grew out of the strong wind. The land shrank quickly the further we paddled. Two hours and six miles out, the wind began blowing hard. Three to five foot waves approached from the open seas.

Another hour passed. We were half way, and no land was visible in any direction. Our only navigation was a line of buoys that disappeared over the horizon. This was where things got nasty. An endless supply of four to six foot waves rocked the boats from our left side. To keep the canoes straight, we could only paddle on one side. To stop paddling was certainly not an option; doing so the boat would capsize. For hours I watched Robert disappear behind wave after wave, relieved to see him still going each time. Spotting land gave us some hope, but it was still hours away.

Robert looked over at me and yelled, "This is crazy!"

We then burst into laughter. A Coast Guard vessel passed in the distance several times doing patrols.

When we could see land a little clearer, we picked our landing spot and focused on just making it. We were hungry, thirsty and needed to relieve ourselves, but had no way to satisfy the urges. We landed behind a jetty in a protected cove in front of several beach homes in Port O'Connor. We both relieved our bladders right in front of God and everybody then began to chug down water from our supply. Looking into Robert's boat I noticed nothing was tied in. After bringing it up to him he said, "If I dumped, it was all gone any ways."

It had taken six and a half hours to successfully survive the 19-mile crossing in open canoes, nothing short of a miracle.

A man walking up the beach gave us a puzzled look, and asked, "You crossed Matagorda in those little things?"

"Sure did," I responded.

Scratching his head, the man invited us to his home for Thanksgiving dinner a day early. His name was Joe, and his family treated us to a full turkey dinner with all the trimmings. It was just what we needed after the brutal crossing.

After days of slamming the character of barge pilots, we found out Joe was one of them. After hearing some of our barge problems, he jokingly said he was surprised we weren't kicking his butt. We laughed and said that now we have proof that not all barge captains are the same. After a great, unexpected meal, we paddled out around the jetty and back into the high seas to reach the protected waters of the Intra-Coastal Waterway and made camp.

The water was considerably clearer. That night flat bottom boats propelled by tiny plane propellers carried fishermen through the shallows as they gigged flounder from under bright halogen lights mounted across the bows.

The next day was Thanksgiving. We moved our camp from the fishing hot spot to a quieter location and took the day off. A phone was only a short paddle away, so we took advantage of it to call our families.

The very next day we battled 30mph headwinds. To make progress, we waded through the shallow water pulling our boats along the canal. A mama porpoise with her pup followed along side. If we stopped, they stopped. The whole event continued for hours. It made the miserable 8-mile canoe drag truly an amazing one. After hours of entertainment, mama and pup suddenly disappeared out of our lives with a flip of their tails.

We camped at Charlie's Bait Camp that night. It was out in the middle of nowhere, but a lot of fishermen used the camp. An older couple there served us a chicken fried steak dinner with all the trimmings. It sure beat the Ramen noodle dinner we had planned. Later we discovered that bird watchers use the camp as well. They come to see wetland birds, as well as, the whooping cranes that wintered there.

The salt water was still taking a toll on our gear and our bodies. We were unable to bathe in fresh water and had developed salt burns on various parts of our bodies. The rusted gear was a serious problem. Our stoves died simultaneously on San Jose Island, and nearly all our food needed to be cooked. To make things worse there was no firewood. For supper, Robert dined on catsup and crackers while I feasted on pistachio pudding. That evening as the sun set we could see the lights of Rockport, Texas, glistening across the bay.

With stomach growling, I looked through binoculars across the bay in search of a fast food sign. I told Robert, "If I see a McDonald's sign, I'm paddling across this bay tonight!" Tormented by mosquitoes, I gave up and crawled into my tent.

For weeks Robert's tent zipper had been broken. To survive he used duct tape each night for repairs. My zipper was now broken and

Robert was at the end of his roll. There was no way to secure the flap, so I surrendered to the swarms of mosquitoes.

The next morning, we crossed the bay to Rockport. Kevin, at Bayfront Cottages, gave us three days for $95. We couldn't afford it, but did it anyway. The cottages were like little apartments, exactly what we needed. We rinsed the salt off our gear, did laundry, showered and best of all, Kevin brought us steaks, hot and still on the grill.

We decided it would be smart to get off the salt water as soon as possible. Studying maps, we realized the Nueces River was an option. The Nueces dumped into the Gulf of Mexico at Corpus Christi, Texas, and it was only 50 miles away. We could paddle up the Nueces, then portage to the Rio Grande River. With our route determined, we picked up a new stove, packed our gear and continued the journey.

Two days later we crossed Corpus Christi Bay and landed next to the USS Lexington Museum On The Bay, a berthed aircraft carrier, in Corpus Christi. Channel 3 came down to do an interview. It was the best one so far. When finished, we paddled up and made camp at the mouth of the Nueces River.

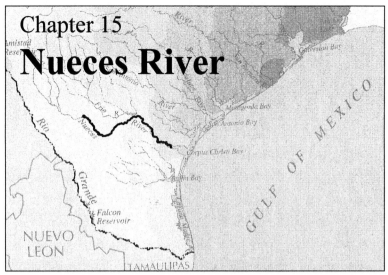

Chapter 15
Nueces River

December 5, 2000 – January 22, 2001

The first night on the Nueces River, a small raccoon came into camp. It seemed to have no fear as it walked right up to me while I ate supper. I took out a cracker and offered it to the small animal that was only 18 inches away. Almost humanlike, it sat down on its back paws and waved as if to say, "Come on just give me the cracker." After a few minutes, I tossed the cracker at its feet. The raccoon picked it up and ate it like a sandwich. Patiently it sat waiting for another cracker. I offered it another cracker from my hand but it still refused, repeating the same hand gestures. Finally I gave in again and threw the cracker at its feet. Slowly, it ate the cracker like it was a delicacy. I left a few more crackers for the raccoon and retired to my newly repaired tent.

Eight miles upstream we came to a public river access where we met Beverly. Her brother offered to take us, not far from where we were, to a local grocery store to get supplies. When we returned, we talked a while with Beverly and her husband, James, who invited us to stay in their guesthouse as long as we wanted.

The next day Beverly ran us around town. We stopped in at Channel 3 to get a copy of the interview from two days before. The reporter who covered the story gave us a tour of the station. It was interesting to watch how everything worked behind the scenes. While the interview was being copied at the main control panel, people began to gather around and listen to our stories. All of the sudden, all the display screens went blank. Robert and I had caused a distraction, leaving nobody at the controls. One man looked up at the blank panel and screamed, "Oh no!"

He then slammed a tape in and started pushing buttons like the world depended on it. With everything back to normal, we quickly moved along with the copy of the interview we had come for and said our goodbyes as the reporter led us out.

When we arrived back at the house, The Corpus Christi Caller-Times, the local newspaper, was waiting for an interview. We hauled my canoe down to the water and posed for pictures while answering all the familiar questions. We stayed another night, enjoyed a home cooked meal and watched some rented movies.

The next morning Beverly took us for breakfast. The restaurant was packed with people reading their morning papers. Everywhere we looked we saw our faces on the cover of the local section. People would look down, then look at us, then look back at the paper, and then back at us again. This went on until a waitress walked up with a newspaper and asked for an autograph for her daughter. The whole room watched and listened in as we talked over breakfast. Several people wished us good luck as we left.

Back at the river, Beverly sent us off with a bunch of herbal products from her local business, "Back To Basics." We steadily moved upriver passing riverside homes and were met again by James, Beverly and family. They brought us lunch and a final farewell.

That same day upriver a naked woman ran out of her house and hollered, "I saw you on TV!" and ran back inside. It was like she forgot she was naked.

Not far below Corpus Christi Lake, an hour after sunset, I heard the familiar sound of a paddle being worked through the water. I told Robert that someone was coming and he jumped out of his tent.

By starlight we could see a man paddling down river in a kayak. I said, "Howdy", and the man about fell out of his boat. We asked if he was okay and if he needed anything. The man responded no, that he and the people behind him had got a late start and now they were stuck paddling in the dark. We wished him good luck as he paddled off into the darkness.

A good half-hour later several more kayaks were approaching in the complete darkness. I greeted them with, "Howdy", and one of them responded, "We're there!"

Robert then informed them, "No you're not."

It was a pitiful sight. They were all lost and scared. Their only gear besides boats, paddles and water jugs was a tiny little flashlight. The lost group asked where we were and where we had put in. Not trying to sound like smart-alecks I responded, "Texas and Kansas City."

One of the women in the group began to panic and started screaming, "Tell us where we are!"

We had as much of a clue as the kayakers did, never being there before. We tried to calm her down and offered food and water. They accepted water and asked, "Where did you really put in?"

"We really put in at Kansas City, and we really don't know where we are," I responded.

One of the men in the group said thanks and then urged the group to move on down river.

The next day we reached Corpus Christi Lake Dam, and as we did, a very loud siren began to blow. It was a warning to those down below that the dam was about to release water. The river began to rise quickly. What timing!

We portaged two miles around the dam following the shortest route to the water. Reaching a resort gate, we were informed that it would cost $20 each to launch our canoes. We told the gatekeeper we simply wanted to launch and go, never to be seen again. She called her boss and explained the situation. He agreed to a fee of $5 each. To avoid several more miles of portaging, we paid the fee. Shortly after arriving at the water, her boss showed up and apologized for any inconvenience and offered a place to camp at no charge. We stayed the night and left first thing the next morning.

We stopped at the Camp Bell Marina across the lake. It was closed for the winter but Dick, the new owner, insisted that we make camp at no charge. We went to the store in Lagardo, just up the road. While there, we met one of the locals who took us to a bar and grill for a couple of drinks. We met a man named Billy, who gave us a ride back to camp. Before departing he gave us some supplies to help us up the river.

Not five minutes had passed back at camp when we spotted a wall of wind coming across the lake out of the north. Seeing it coming, we jumped in our tents. Strong wind mixed with cold rain and snow instantly flattened our tents around us. At that moment the reality of winter was in our faces. The brunt of the storm died, but the chill remained.

Fortunately in South Texas, winter doesn't stick around long and in two days we were off again. Leaving Camp Bell, the lake was dead calm, blanketed with thick fog. We zigzagged our way through dead standing trees that once thrived along the river's edge now half-submerged below the surface of Mathis Lake.

Robert's instincts conflicted with my GPS while searching for our way back onto the Nueces River. We decided to ignore the GPS and follow Robert's hunch. Thanks to his navigational skills, we found what we were looking for, and it saved us several miles of paddling off-course.

While eating lunch near the confluence of the Frio and Nueces Rivers, we spotted several nice pieces of petrified wood. Leaving the Nueces,  we turned up the Frio River pulling our canoes over three small logjams arriving at a pool of water below a nice waterfall.

My mom, and Aunts Helen and Karen, arrived from Kansas to meet us for Christmas at Tips Park near Three Rivers, Texas. Two guys named Doug who lived in campers at the campground offered to watch our gear while we went to stay at nearby Choke Canyon Lake. Herds of deer, turkey and javelina (wild pigs) walked fearlessly only inches away. It was awesome for wildlife viewing and photography and was like a petting zoo with no fences.

During the visit, we took a road trip to San Antonio where we toured the famous Riverwalk and, of course, the Alamo. The week flew by and sadly I said my goodbyes to my family, back at Tips Park, where the Dougs were watching our gear.

Beverly drove up and took us back to Corpus Christi to celebrate New Years. Traditionally we would spend New Years paddling a river. This would be the first New Years Day in a long time we did not follow tradition. We celebrated the night at a local club and returned to Tips Park two days later.

Thus far, the Nueces wasn't much trouble, so we made good mileage with moderate effort. However, leaving Tips Park, all that changed. More and more debris became big obstacles to overcome. Logjams were the major problem. Each day the logjams became larger and more dangerous. Normally we would single handedly move our own gear and canoe, determined to stay independent of each other. However, under the extreme conditions of the Nueces, we began to help one another move gear over and around obstacles. Robert's brother, Kenny, had given him a sturdy folding saw for Christmas. That little saw was a major contributing factor to climbing the Nueces River.

The landscape changed now that we were farther away from the coast. The riverbanks had become vertical mud walls, some several meters high. The Nueces River Valley was flat and over grown with impassable thorn brush. After days of cutting paths through and over logjams, we discussed retreating. Knowing what it took to get where we were, we knew what it would take to go back. Walking out was not an option. Coming to the conclusion that we had already passed the point of no return, we put it out of our minds and continued upriver.

The Nueces had become the biggest challenge of our lives. Each morning we decided who would take the lead. As we approached each logjam, we would ram the bow up onto the twisted tree mass enough to hold the canoe in place. Climbing to the front of the canoe, we would climb out on top of the logjam and just pull the gear over the top if we could. Unfortunately it was not always that easy. Some of the time it was necessary to basically tunnel through, always being very careful not to drop the saw. About every 10 logjams we would surrender the saw to the other man due to complete exhaustion.

Several times while sitting on top of the logjams sawing, the entire logjam would break free putting us in even more danger. To escape, we had to pry the canoe off, hop into it, climb over gear, grab our paddle and scramble for the closest shore to let the mangled mess pass by. This had to be done quickly to prevent being crushed and pulled under the previous logjam we had just passed over. Riding a logjam definitely got the heart pumping.

Logjams were not the only hazards. Two-dozen barbwire and mesh game-fences had to be crossed. Several fences we had to unwire then respectfully put back how we found them. Dams, all 14 of them - except Corpus Christi Lake, had to be portaged the old fashioned way. We were required to unload the gear and carry it on our backs over the rugged terrain. Many of them were 15-20 feet high making it difficult to get the 400 pounds each we were hauling up and over. Above the dam was nice, flat paddling for a ways, instead of the constant 3 to 5 mile an hour current we normally had to battle.

Miles from civilization, I had been complaining about a broken tooth that was cutting into my tongue. The cut had caused my tongue to swell making it difficult to eat, drink or even talk. Unable to bear the pain any longer, I took out some pliers and snapped the tooth off at the gum line. I then rinsed out the remaining shards with water. With the amount of relief it provided, I wished I had done it sooner.

Despite the physical torture, we had found a wildlife paradise. With no humans for miles, the wildlife seemed almost tame. Uncountable turkey and quail flourished in the area. It was not uncommon to see half-a-dozen owls roosting in a tree. Setting a line off the back of my canoe at night almost always provided catfish to eat. We saw deer at every bend. Due to the abundance of deer, I told Robert that there had to be mountain lion feeding in the area.

One day I saw a large deer with white spots run off into the brush. It resembled a fawn, but had to be over 250 pounds. Later we discovered it was an exotic deer called an Axis. Hunting camps in the area introduced them years ago and now they had become overpopulated. Hunters were allowed to kill and eat them year round with no special permits.

Long stretches of the river had Live Oak trees that reached out over the river touching one another across the water. This was something we had never before seen. These Live Oaks were ancient in appearance and gave the remote area a mystical feel.

One day approaching a logjam, Robert jumped out and was about to start sawing when I spotted an alligator. Whispering to Robert, I warned him that there was an alligator next to him. Looking around he asked, "Where?"

"Right beside you," I replied.

Robert looked again and spotted the camouflaged three-foot lizard right next to him. "Oh!" he said, putting a couple more feet between him and the alligator.

I looked at Robert and said that I was going to wrestle it. Robert smiled and said, "Go for it. He's going to kick your butt!"

I had wanted to wrestle an alligator since Louisiana and now was my chance. First I took some pictures then slowly crept up  within three feet of the large reptile. Like a bolt of lightening it came to life and dove into the river. Robert laughed and said, "Jump in there and get 'em!"

I declined. We saw several alligator slides, some indicated 10ft+ reptiles. Thankfully it was winter; the alligators were moving slowly and the cottonmouths were hibernating. We firmly believed that if anyone attempted this section during the warmer months they would perish.

Listening to headphones in my tent one night, I heard Robert screaming my name. I turned off the music and said, "What?"

With concern in his voice, Robert said, "There's something out here going to eat us!"

Immediately I grabbed my gun when I heard something moving between our tents. A mountain lion, moaning like it was in heat or pain, had wandered into camp. The lion paced back and forth between our tents for several minutes. Eventually, the lion slowly moved away, still screaming into the night.

Winter camping had several benefits: no bugs, food didn't spoil as quickly and dangerous cold-blooded reptiles were hibernating for the most part. It also had its problems. The daytime highs were around 50 degrees, with the lows being in the 20's. It also rained on us almost daily. Rain, wading and sweat left us soaked from head to toe all day. To prevent suffering from hypothermia we followed the old saying, "If you're cold, you're not working hard enough!" When we took breaks, we only stopped for about 15 minutes or until one of us began to shiver. The harder we worked the warmer we were.

We used the same wet clothes day after day. Each morning during coffee and breakfast, we warmed the wet or frozen clothes next to the fire until they began to

steam. With the canoes fully loaded, we would quickly change into the warm wet clothes and head out before a chill could set in.

After two weeks without seeing anyone, we heard gunshots. Just around the corner we came to a dam with several buildings above it resembling a hunt camp. The sun was setting fast, but we still began the portage.

I went over to the main house, knocked and asked to use their phone. I explained to the man who answered the door that my dad had surgery days ago and that I wanted to call and check on him. The man seemed confused, but handed me the phone anyway. I called home and found out that my dad was okay. The man asked where I had came from and I explained that we had come up the river. I explained that I needed to return to the river and complete portaging before it was too dark.

As we were about to make camp, the owners of the Helgie Hunt Camp told us there had been a cancellation and that we could use one of their cabins at no charge. The accommodations were great. The cabin slept 8 people with a large living room complete with satellite TV and comfortable couches. The first thing we did was warm our bones with hot showers.

The next morning Mr. Helgie told us he had lived there for over 70 years and had never heard of anyone successfully going up or down this section of the river. While we were complaining about the constant rains, he informed us that there had been no water flowing over the dam until a couple of weeks ago. The rain had been a Godsend.

We stayed another day and helped make a couple of hundred pounds of sausage. While sharing stories, Mr. Helgie told us about a couple who had put a canoe in up river to float down. They ended up losing everything and had to walk out. Near death, they were found days later and rescued. Robert and I had just done what no one had ever done before.

We gave our thanks and goodbyes to the Helgie family after a much needed break and moved on. A little over 20 miles up, we came to a gravel road below a collapsed dam. It was the first public road we had seen in over two weeks and we had seen more than our fill of the Nueces River. With 226 miles of the river behind us, we had endured 250 logjams within the last 95 miles alone. The Nueces River was the biggest challenge of our lives thus far. We didn't care how far it was, we were walking to the Rio Grande.

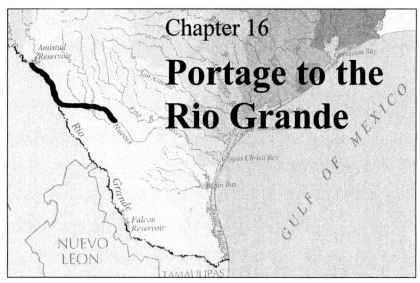

Chapter 16
Portage to the Rio Grande

January 22 – February 16, 2001

We began the long walk to Cotulla, Texas, with 400 pounds of gear each loaded onto our portage carts. Several people stopped to ask, "Just what the heck are you doing?" Some even offered us a ride and looked surprised when the answer was no. It was getting dark with several miles still yet to go. With very little water and food, it was a forced march and we needed to make it to civilization.

The sun had set turning the night air cool. With sweat dripping from our bodies, we began to shiver. Stopping to put on more clothes, we grabbed extra flashlights. The highway had no shoulder. Therefore, with each passing of a vehicle, we were forced to drag the canoes off the highway onto a steep soft shoulder. The task of getting back on the road each time was painful; we had to pick the loaded canoes up and out of the sandy shoulder.

Nearing town we began to see dead animals along the road and not the normal road kill. Dead goats and other farm animals lined the ditches. It seemed like some satanic ritual had occurred along the roadway. We passed a house where several dogs threatened to attack, putting us even more on edge.

Robert was sick and exhausted. Barely able to walk, he refused to stop longer than to just catch his breath.

It was getting pretty late into the night when we saw a car coming up the road spotlighting the fields along it. Two guys pulled up next to Robert shinning the spotlight on him. They were acting very suspicious so I reached down and picked up my loaded rifle. The two guys asked what we were up to and Robert answered by telling the shortest version of our story possible.

The passenger, overwhelmed with excitement, asked for an autograph, insisting, "Make it out to Ricky!" Then they went on to brag about how they were trying to poach deer. We were not impressed with their hunting ethics, and continued on for the lights of Cotulla.

Upon reaching town, we were stopped by a local deputy sheriff. Our firearms were in clear view, which believed was in accordance with the law. The sheriff shined his flashlight over the canoes and saw the guns. Half panicked he screamed, "Cover them up! How long are you going to be in town? Let me see some identification."

While he was running our ID's, Robert and I took turns utilizing the convenience store where we were stopped. The deputy came back from his car and told us not to flash our guns anywhere in town and to keep them concealed. We covered our weapons and moved on.

By now, Robert was extremely sick and could not go on without some rest. We found a cheap motel and got a room. To make things worse, he found out that his Grandpa, Junior Manchester, whom he was very close to, had passed away.

After a days rest, we continued on down the road crossing I-35. Looking north up the interstate, we realized home was just up the road. Pushing away homesickness, we continued on.

Eight miles past Carrizo Springs, Texas, we heard what sounded like a gunshot from behind us. Looking back I saw that my canoe was leaning heavy to one side, having blown a tire. I took off the tire and made a new one by wrapping layer after layer of duct tape around the rim. This only worked for a short distance.

Around dark, a rancher driving off his land, stopped to talk. Hearing my problem he said he would help out. We stashed the gear in some thick mesquite brush and took GPS coordinates. Then we gathered the valuables like journals, cameras, guns and some clothes and accepted a ride in the back of the rancher's pick-up back to a motel in town.

Robert's parents, Kenny and Mary Lou, arrived from Kansas the next day to pick up our guns. We all went looking for a new tire, but nobody in town had one for sale. Several stores offered to order me one that could be delivered within a couple of days.

Our last stop was a Coast to Coast store where we heard the same story. Looking around I spotted the exact sized tire I needed. The problem was it wasn't for sale; it was part of a sales display. I asked the sales clerk if he would sell it to me. Confused by the question, he told me it had been stabbed with an ice pick at least 100 times. I told him that it didn't matter because I had a tube that would fit.

The sales clerk then said, "If you need it that bad, you can just have it." After thanking God and the clerk, we walked out the door excited to be on our way again. Robert's parents dropped us off at the canoes where we quickly went to work.

We said goodbye after giving Ken our guns. Firearms were outlawed in Mexico and just the thought of spending time in a Mexican prison was reason enough to send them home.

After approximately 100 miles of portaging, we arrived at Eagle Pass located on the Rio Grande River. We were a mess; our feet were bruised and bleeding. We had also developed a severe rash on our inner thighs, so bad that scabs had formed. Unable to go on, we got a motel room. Being a border town, we took no chances and dragged the boats and gear into the room with us.

The next morning was Robert's birthday. He celebrated at a restaurant next door, eating a $20 breakfast. The same day, Danny, the motel owner's son stopped by our room. Looking in the open door he said, "You guys live like rock stars!"

He then offered to show us around the area. Always ready for an adventure, we took him up on the offer. Cruising around that night, we somehow ended up back on the Nueces River, further upstream from where we took out. At the river's edge, he told us there was a cool place to hang out just across the river. He then floored it, as we screamed, "NO!"

A wall of water formed in front of the truck. Halfway across the pickup stalled and water rushed into the cab. Robert and I put our feet on the dash and took off our socks and shoes. Water rushed by with great force as we got out of the truck.

We waded to the shore barefooted in the pitch-black darkness of the night. Danny apologized the entire time as we put on our dry shoes. We were at least 70 miles from our gear, stranded in the middle of nowhere at night and not exactly sure of where we were.

Danny apologized even more as we walked up the gravel road. We kept answering back, "Don't worry about it, it's just the Nueces."

After walking awhile, a police car pulled up. We got in and the officer gave us a ride to Danny's parent's home not far away. With no keys to get in, the kid kicked the door in and threw us the remote to the TV and called someone for help. A few minutes later that someone showed up. Danny said he'd be right back with his truck. Not long after they got back, he had the pickup running again. At the same time, his mom arrived and gave Robert and me a ride back to Eagle Pass. Waking up late the next day, the owners gave us another night's stay for free. Needless to say we didn't get the rest we were looking for, but what an adventure!

The next day we went down to the river access. Everyone including the Border Patrol told us to stay out of Mexico. We were told that across this section of border was home to 80% of the inhabitants of Mexico. Looking across the river we spotted a Federale (Mexican policeman) looking at us through binoculars. Suspicious people everywhere, combined with the horror border stories; we decided to research our options. We saw a road on the map that followed parallel to the river. We figured it was safer to follow the road up to Amistad Lake rather than take our chances with the Federales.

North of Eagle Pass we met a man named Warren. He was building a road into a new housing development. After talking awhile, we discovered that he knew Alex Dugas from back in Louisiana. He told us to make camp anywhere we wanted and left a cooler full of cold drinks. The next morning he greeted us with breakfast sandwiches and wished us good luck.

Passing Normandy, Texas, a stray dog began to follow along. It followed us for miles; we couldn't get him to go away. Several people stopped and took pictures. Some even gave Robert and me money, "to help with the cause."

One of the people who stopped said there was another person trying to catch up. As a middle-aged man rode up on a bicycle, the people drove off and the man introduced himself as Calvin. We had lunch with him and refused to feed the dog. Finally the dog got the hint and went back in the direction he came from.

Calvin had been traveling for a year and a half on his bicycle. He was working on his book called M.U.N. (Modern Urban Nomad). He gave us $20 and said he would pray for us. On up the road we came to a roadside restaurant and now having $20 we went inside for food. Something other than Ramen noodles! Once inside we saw Calvin again. We shared another meal with Calvin, swapping stories from each other's adventures. The locals listening in asked several questions. Calvin asked if he could tag along with us for awhile and we readily agreed.

That night we camped under the Tequesquite Creek Bridge. I awoke in the early morning light to the sound of splashing in the creek. Looking up, two illegal aliens were running through the camp. I hollered over to the other guys, "We got company!" The illegals ran even faster, scaling a tall fence designed to keep them out of the U.S.

The next day we said goodbye to Calvin. He insisted we look him up when we got to San Diego.

We arrived in Del Rio and stayed in a motel three nights thanks to a fan who wished to remain anonymous. Calvin somehow found us again. We offered him a hot shower before leaving once again. I partied with some locals at a nearby club where a nice lady named Ms. Jenny showed me how to Texas two-step.

Leaving Del Rio, healed from our ailments, we arrived at beautiful Lake Amistad. The 165-mile portage was over. Oh the joy! We were finally back on the water.

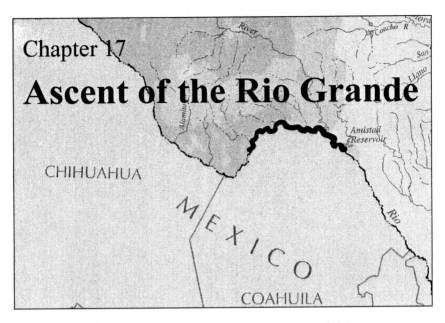

Chapter 17
Ascent of the Rio Grande

February 16 – March 14, 2001

For months people had been talking about the paddling opportunities available along the Texas-Mexico border. I called several commercial river outfitters asking about river conditions and other area information. After explaining our plans to paddle upstream, all responded, "How are you going to get past the rapids?"

After extensive research, we concluded that no one had ever successfully climbed this section of river, or at least it had not been recorded. Attempts made by Spanish explorers were prevented by Native Americans living in the area, as well as, the rugged terrain and lack of resources. Undeterred, we paddled out onto Lake Amistad. The feeling was surreal as we glided across the beautiful, crystal clear water; very unlike the muddy Rio Grande that feeds the reservoir.

Happy to be back on the water, we made camp early. The next morning the wind was blowing hard and crashing waves onto the shore where we were camped. Wind-bound for the day, we passed the time hiking and catching up journals. Further exploration of the bluffs lining the lake revealed ancient artwork from past civilizations.

While on the lake we saw leisure boating, scuba divers, fishermen, houseboats and families enjoying the lakeside parks. The lake offered beautiful desert vistas in every direction. The many outdoor activities, as well as the beauty, made it a great place to visit.

Canyon walls now clearly marked our trail as we made our way off the lake and onto the muddy waters of the Rio Grande River. The dam downriver caused large amounts of silt from the Rio to be deposited on the lakebed over the years. Due to a ten year drought, the lake recessed exposing the silt beds where trees had taken root and were thriving in the riverbed creating navigational problems. In a few

spots, it was even difficult to identify the main channel.

Caves dotted the canyon walls and at times several dozen could be viewed in each direction. Exploring Panther Cave, which was gated off from the public, we photographed pictographs left behind by the civilizations that once thrived there. Some dated as far back as 8,000 years. Not far was Pink Cave named for the obvious reason: it was pink. It was easily accessible and had several faded pictographs that could be studied up close.

Just below the mouth of the Pecos River we came to Parida Cave. We made camp next to the river and climbed up the steep rocky terrain to explore it. Climbing the bank it seemed as though we had stepped back it time. I believed this location was the home

PARIDA CAVE
N 29° 41.216'
W 101° 22.300'

of a head Chief. From this vantage point was the most beautiful view from a cave either of us had ever seen. Looking up river was the Pecos, across the river was a tributary coming in from Mexico, and downstream there was a full view for defense. Parida was protected from weather and enemy attack by a large overhang. Indian artwork blanketed the cave walls, some very detailed. A National Park Service

sign described the importance of not disturbing the artifacts. However, several holes were present where people had robbed what they pleased.

With all the hundreds of caves in plain view, we had to pick and choose what to explore, if we were to make any mileage. One cave high up on the side of a bluff caught our eye. Climbing over 100 vertical feet above the river we discovered an overhang that appeared to have not been disturbed by humans. No pictographs were visible and the floor was perfectly smooth, covered in goat dung.

Guessing that it had never been named, we dubbed it Goat Cave. Despite the extreme difficulty in reaching the cave, we were rewarded with a breathtaking view overlooking the canyon lined Rio Grande. This section had so many holes in the canyon walls, I believed it would take a lifetime to explore them all.

Our progress was about 10 miles a day going upriver. We spent our breaks exploring overhangs and caves as we went. Climbing the river, we had developed a steady routine. Each morning began with coffee and a quick breakfast, followed by breaking camp no later than nine in the morning. Daily we paddled hard against the swift current. When climbing a riffle or rapid, we were forced to wade up along the river's edge against the even more powerful current, all the while trying to stay out of Mexico.

One day we heard the hum of a boat motor coming from down stream. Hearing the boat long before we saw it, two men in a johnboat flew by. We guessed the men to be drug runners or law enforcement because they sure were not fishermen. The boat motor came to a stop not far away and we paddled up to the boat.

Two men came down a narrow path looking directly at us. The men were armed and by now Robert and I could see they had to be some type of law enforcement. We introduced ourselves and the strangers did the same, pulling out Border Patrol badges. After telling them where we were from, one looked surprised. It turned out he had graduated high school with Robert, but neither remembered meeting.

The agents warned that most of the people that we may encounter along the river were probably illegals crossing or drug runners. They also repeated several times, "Stay out of Mexico". They informed us that the small trail that we were standing on was known for illegal activity, but that it also led to a cool overhang not far away. Exploring it, we found the floor covered in flint pieces indicating years of flint napping. No longer home to anyone, the agents claimed that it was a regular hangout for drug-runners.

Exploring as we went, we discovered an amazing sight. Springs covered with silt had formed pools that resembled small volcanoes. Out of the pools boiled sand and water creating quicksand. We measured them to be about 4 feet deep. I had not seen anything like it since being a child at Yellowstone National Park. These pools appeared dangerous enough to trap and drown a person.

We had run out of food and were anxiously looking for the next place on our route to re-supply. Spotting some minnow buckets full of goldfish along the bank, we knew we must be close. Following a narrow 4x4 trail, I walked to the nearest house and met Jack and Wilmuth. Jack and I picked up Robert and drove into Langtry, Texas, for supplies. The only store in town with groceries was a gas station. We bought most of what they had in stock, but it was only enough for maybe a week's rations.

We also visited the famous Judge Roy Bean Visitors Center to absorb some local history of the area. Jack, an author, gave us advice on publishing a book about our adventure over lunch.

I ordered a double cheeseburger at a local restaurant in town. Sitting down at the table, I noticed there was only one beef patty on the bun. Returning to the counter to complain that there was only one patty, the cashier responded, "There's two pieces of cheese."

I thought he was joking, but he wasn't. I told him that in my travels around the planet, this was the only place a double cheeseburger didn't come with two pieces of meat.

Returning to the table, Jack only smiled like this event was a local joke. We now refer to Langtry as home of the "doublecheese" burger. We returned to the river the way we came and moved on with inadequate supplies.

Above Langtry we came upon the first of several large rapids we would ascend on the Rio. Fighting the current, we waded up through the swift water with the canoes in tow, carefully keeping our footing to prevent being swept downstream.

The hills and valleys were covered in wildflowers giving the air the scent of potpourri as we approached an unoccupied fishing camp. The camp had several permanent structures that were as secure as a bank vault. The steel structures were built with intense ingenuity and had all the comforts of home despite the extreme remoteness.

Around the perimeter were huts fashioned out of river cane. We made ourselves at home in the cane huts, after bathing in the river. The camp had a windmill where we were able to fill our water jugs. The fresh water was a true delight from the nasty river water we had been forced to drink. That night, I spent my 27th birthday celebrating with a Snickers bar for supper.

Due to lack of food supplies, we had to push hard from sunup to sundown. Looking at one another, it was obvious that we had lost a lot of weight. Since the beginning of the trip, we had shed over 40 pounds each. I was already thin when we left Kansas City and often wondered if I was going to live. Pure stubborn determination to succeed pushed us on. Despite the harsh conditions, we were having the time of their lives.

Through this section of river it was obvious that the area was a hotspot for Mexicans crossing over. Clothes and trash covered in Spanish writing dotted the banks. Some of the illegals used inner tubes to float across. We found this strange because in so many places a person could just wade across. Looking through some debris, Robert found a Green Card that had just expired only a few days past.

The river changed even more just below the Dryden River access. Larger rapids presented even more hazardous conditions. As we waded along the edge of the rapids, small boulders rolled out from under our feet while we towed the canoes by their bowlines. Several times we were dangerously close to capsizing the boats and falling into the turbulent rapids. It was a rush!

Six miles above Dryden, a popular takeout for the Lower Canyons commercial float trip, we came upon the first people we had seen in a week. A group of twenty or so high school students, accompanied by chaperones, were camped in Mexico and were running around with no concern. The chaperones informed us that it was legal and customary to camp and play on the Mexico side.

For months we had been told, "Stay out of Mexico." Robert and I were furious and very disappointed. For weeks we had passed-up the opportunity to explore very appealing areas, intriguing formations and captivating landscapes in constant fear of the consequences of stepping into Mexico.

The group invited us to camp and stay for supper. We joined them, without hesitation, for an excellent meal. The group of young people from Louisiana was very impressive. Hanging out around the campfire, the students shared stories of the section of river we were about to enter. I found them to be bright teenagers, all with very promising futures.

The next morning a chaperone gave Robert a detailed guide book for the Lower Canyons. This book described: side canyons, where to find springs for water and bathing, locations of rapids, hiking trails, popular camp sites, brief historic facts and was loaded with other helpful information.

The group told us to help ourselves to any of the food they had left because they were going home and didn't want it to go to waste.

With only two days worth of food left and at least one more week of travel before any hope of civilization, this was a Godsend. Loaded up with two more weeks of food and full of excitement and relief we continued upriver.

Days later we stopped for lunch at a private river access called Bone Watering. The wind began to blow hard as dark clouds passed overhead in the deep canyon. Preparing for a strong storm, we made camp. However, the storm passed and the skies cleared so we tore down camp to continue upriver. Just as we were about to move on, an old Chevy Blazer pulling a trailer drove down the extremely steep access road towards the water. A middle-aged man and woman got out and began unloading a strange looking boat from the trailer.

"What's that?" I asked.

The man responded, "It's a hovercraft."

He introduced himself as Pete McKaskle and asked where we put in. I told him Kansas City and that we were paddling upriver. Pete was excited, and said, "I got to shake your hand."

He then offered to take us for a ride in the hovercraft. Accepting his offer, one at a time we went "flying" through the deep cut limestone bluffs. The vessel hovered over rapids and gravel bars with ease.

Pete and his wife Sandra invited us up to their fish camp for supper and warm beds to sleep in. The next morning they fed us a real breakfast before giving us a ride back to the river. Pete told us he'd be fishing upstream and would see us again.

Later that day we hiked into Big Thicket Voyagers Canyon. Some distance back into the beautiful water carved canyon, we found a double-door cave showing years of human activity. Smoke stains tarnished the ceiling and there was evidence of flint harvesting on the ceiling and walls. Like good conservationists, we took lots of pictures and left only footprints.

At the mouth of the canyon, Pete and Sandra "flew" up in the hovercraft to bring us sodas and snacks on their way to do some fishing upstream. Above San Francisco Canyon we ran into Pete and Sandra returning home. Pete unloaded their remaining sodas and said he would meet us at Heath Canyon, the put-in for the Lower Canyon week long float trip.

Upriver we arrived at Panther Rapid. We scaled the bluff along side it to scout. We discovered it would be a major obstacle to portage around. To save time, we decided to take our chances and "line" up the rapids, floating the canoes behind us while climbing along the rivers edge.

The last section of rapids proved to be the most difficult. We had reached the steep bluff wall and were forced to hold the bowline of the canoe in our teeth as we rock climbed our way up the U.S. side. It took everything we had to reach the top of the rapids. Now surrounded by rapids and up against the bluff, we had come to a dead end. From this point we would have to ferry across the river.

One at a time, Robert first, we had to jump into the canoe and paddle with all our strength into the swift current. Missing a stroke with the paddle, the boat would be sucked backward into the boulder-infested rapid below. With a high chance of loosing everything, we made the daring leap across to the safety of a gentle eddy. It was an adrenaline rush we had not felt for awhile.

A hundred miles - as the crow flies – and days from the nearest hospital, made us question whether or not we should be taking such risks this far out in the bush. Still slightly shaken, we made camp just above the rapids.

The students from Louisiana had told us to be sure to hike the Burro Bluff trail for the view of a lifetime. Arriving at the base of the cliff, we found several rafts tied up at the rivers edge. The group had already set up camp and hiked up. After changing into dry boots, Robert and I began the ascent. Along the steep trail were signs of flint harvesting, as well as Indian artifacts. On top of the 900-foot bluff we met a group of a dozen people enjoying the view.

From this vantage point we could see for miles into Mexico's topography. The river had cut through the landscape leaving behind layers of carved limestone mountains. Overwhelmed by its splendor we took several pictures. From this elevation, our canoes were barely visible at the base of Upper Madison Falls, a huge rapid on the Rio.

As all but three from the group descended the mountain, their trip leader invited Robert and me to stop by their camp. The photographer remained behind. While talking with him, I discovered he was there on assignment from National Geographic and told him of some great photo ops down river. I also advised him to keep his eyes open for Indian artifacts along the trail leading back to his camp. On our way down, we spotted a nice flint scrapper and marked it with an arrow made of dead yucca shoots for the remaining people coming down.

Arriving at the water, the leader of their group was patiently waiting at their camp across the river. We paddled over and introduced ourselves more formally. The leader's name was Ian and beside him was his right hand woman, Patricia. His company, The River League, was based out of Vancouver, British Columbia. They were guiding a National Geographic team, as well as some other tourists from up north. Ian invited us to stay for supper and we readily accepted.

Before going into their camp, we portaged Upper Madison Falls. To complete this undertaking required emptying the boats and dragging them over boulders larger than cars. In two more trips, we packed the rest of the gear over the same boulders. Once the portage was completed, we made camp and bathed in the river.

Walking into The River League's camp presented a complete surprise. The well-organized guides provided comfortable seating for everyone around the campfire. The kitchen was unbelievable. Somehow they had packed a complete gourmet kitchen into the wilderness, and from it was a delicious aroma hovering throughout the camp. Robert and I introduced ourselves to the folks around the fire as our hosts finished preparing supper for the group.

As we sat around the fire talking, one of the women in the group, half buzzed on wine, went on and on, "Do you guys know what you've done?" She pointed to one of the men, "You! You're a writer for National Geographic. Come over here and write this down."

Douglas Chadwick, well known for his writing, took down our story. He asked Robert why we were doing this, and he motioned toward the river, and said, "You don't need a reason to be on a river, do you?" Doug later used Robert's quote in his book called *Exploring America's Wild and Scenic Rivers*.

The photographer came back down with a guide and joined the party. I asked him if he saw the artifact that was marked for him. Describing how it was marked, he walked away disappointed for missing it. He then filled his glass with wine and sat down next to the fire.

Robert and I shared stories over a fantastic supper. While the food was being put away, the photographer brought out his guitar and began to play. A guitar, campfire and great company along the beautiful Rio Grande; life could not be better.

Catfish were not commonly thought of as food in Canadian waters. Patricia asked if we ate catfish and how to clean them. Hearing much talk of forest protection that evening, I jokingly said, "You take that ol' catfish and nail him to a tree."

Before I could go on, the whole group simultaneously took an audible deep breath with surprised looks on their faces. I joked, "I can't help my redneck ways," and they all began to laugh. I then continued, "Down here, I just skin them on a rock."

We sang and talked until one in the morning.

The next morning I checked my fishing line on the way over to their camp for coffee and breakfast. I had caught a four-pound flathead catfish and took it to their camp to show off lunch for the day. Some of the people had never seen a flathead before and took pictures and video to document the experience.

After taking a group photo and saying our goodbyes, the group prepared to depart. We returned to our camp upstream, finished packing and moved on.

That day at the top of Rodeo Rapid we met another group of people. Their guide asked where we had put in and Robert told her Kansas City. She responded "You're full of crap!" Convincing her otherwise, she then congratulated us with a high five introducing herself as Taz.

One of the ladies in the group, of seventy or so years of age, ran Rodeo Rapid in an inflatable kayak. The rapid swallowed her up and threw her out of the boat. Only a few minutes later she was back at the top of the rapid determined to try again. On her second attempt, she ran it successfully and was cheered on by everyone for her success. Before parting ways, Taz said she would look for us again upriver.

Camping on an island that night, we awoke to something splashing in the water. My first instinct was that illegals were coming into camp. I climbed out of my tent into the darkness and remembered setting a fishing line off the back of my canoe. The noise turned out to be an

eight-pound channel cat. I gave Robert my camera to snap my picture with the fish and then released it and went back to sleep.

The next day we climbed several rapids through wild geological terrain and arrived at Hot Springs Rapid. This had been a resting-place for the wayward traveler for many years. Bathing tubs made from hand laid stones had been built there. It felt great soaking our sore muscles in the hot water. We also washed our clothes below the tubs in the warm 85-degree water that billowed right out of the ground.

The next morning we started the day battling the longest rapid we had encountered thus far. For the remainder of the day we fought a

40mph headwind. The wind was so powerful it created large whitecaps that threatened to fill the boats. We made camp early that afternoon out of sheer frustration.

Making up for lost time we left at dawn and soon arrived at Rock House. The landmark was the entrance to the Lower Canyons section of the Rio Grande for paddlers traveling downstream. We were leaving the canyon system and entering a more open valley desert terrain. The cows that grazed along the mountainside looked like ants.

After exploring the Rock House ruins, we moved on passing several hot springs. We came to Balancing Rock where two deer were grazing along the river. Balancing Rock was quite a sight. The huge squared off boulder balanced on one corner seeming to defy gravity.

One day's travel before reaching Heath Canyon river access, we met several groups of people heading down river. Each group we encountered gave us cold drinks. Going upstream we were able to see how many people were using the river. Going downstream, it would have appeared as though we had the river to ourselves. Most of the people that day greeted us by saying, "You're going the wrong way!"

Ducks flew overhead from upriver indicating that someone was coming. Around the bend came three hovercrafts. Pete and his friends stopped by to see how we were doing. They brought food and cold drinks for us on their way to go fishing.

Later that day, Pete and his friends stopped by on their way back to Heath Canyon to show off their catch for the day. In the bottoms of their boats were several large catfish.

Just below the river access we came across two 18-year-old guys in an extremely overloaded canoe. There was a 250-pound guy in the front and 150-pound guy in the back. Gear was stacked so high that the guy in the back could not even see over it. On top of the gear were four, six gallon jugs of water, weighing about 200 pounds, putting the center of gravity much higher than it should have been.

I asked if I could take a picture and cheerfully, they posed for the picture not knowing why. I asked, "Do you even know what's down river? You will never make it like that."

The young men explained that they were caring gear for two other people in their group. Explaining the dangers downstream, we convinced the young men to pull over and re-pack the canoe for their own safety.

We unloaded the canoe on a gravel bar where Robert and I showed them the proper way to pack gear. We dumped out part of their water, leaving them with 12 gallons. Concerned about having enough water, we assured them that there was an abundance of springs and marked them on the map. We also gave them our bleach and explained how to treat the spring water to make it safer to drink. Repacked, we prayed that they would come out on the other end okay, and sent them on their way.

At Heath Canyon, Pete put us up for the night in one of the rooms for rent. We met several people there. One of the men, a champion canoe racer named Tom, personally knew Steven Landick, who had the record that Robert and I were chasing. Tom's family and friends were down to float Boquious Canyon, the next canyon upstream. They were dropping off their shuttle vehicle and grabbing a bite to eat.

After a much needed break, we portaged our canoes back to the river. A small crowd of people walked along with us. Some took pictures, while others just silently gazed at us in amazement. The whole scene looked like a parade that grew as we portaged back to where we had taken out. At the Boquillas take-out and put-in for the Lower Canyons, the group all wished us good luck and safe travels while we repacked our boats. A few even followed along the bank a ways, taking pictures while cheering us on.

The Boquillas section was 33 miles long. At camp a few miles up, we realized we had forgotten to fill our water jugs. Normally, we would just bleach some water and move on, but we had given away the only bleach we had to the young men downstream. We decided to just worry about it in the morning.

At dawn we awoke to a miracle. At the rivers edge in front of our camp was a brand new 2-½ gallon jug of water. We couldn't believe our eyes. The label wasn't even faded from the harsh desert sun and the safety seal was still intact. We thanked God for constantly watching over us and broke camp. I put the jug up on the bow of my canoe to see if anyone would claim it. No one ever did.

Not far upriver we caught a man literally with his pants down. His group had set up the "room with a view" downstream from camp, never expecting anyone to be paddling up river. He quickly donned his pants and walked back to his camp. When the rest of the group spotted us, they looked to their friend who was blushing. It gave them all a good laugh as Robert and I paddled by.

The next group was Tom, the canoe racer, and his daughter's friends on college spring break. The girls asked several questions over lunch. One of them was kind of an airhead, and asked with a Valley Girl voice, "Why are you wearing boots? Like, how are you going to get you're feet tan?"

Several of the group rolled their eyes and motioned with their hands to ignore the question. We were no strangers to dumb questions, but this one was new.

One of the hardest things we had found about the trip was explaining what we were doing. "A tan won't do me any good if I have no feet." I responded.

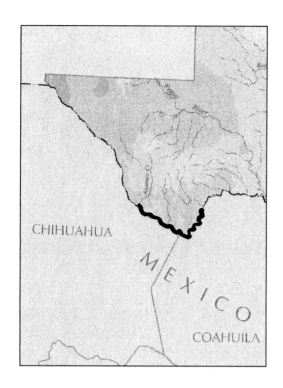

Chapter 18
Big Bend

March 14 –
April 10, 2001

B attling tough headwinds, we inched our way between the 800-foot canyon walls of Boquillas Canyon. Now we were in Big Bend National Park, one of the largest, most secluded National Parks in the United States. The beautiful canyon was one of the most popular float trips in Big Bend. We were passed regularly now with the words, "You're going the wrong way."

Coming out of the canyon we saw a crowd of people in Mexico getting on burros to ride into the Mexican village of Boquillas. Tourists could eat authentic Mexican food, drink at the local cantina and shop for souvenirs.

Not wanting to leave our gear alone, we traveled a short distance further to Rio Grande Village, a BBNP visitor center and camping

facility. We made camp and went looking for supplies, most of which we were able to obtain at the general store.

We had a surprise visitor back at camp. It was Taz, the river guide we had met in the Lower Canyons. She came to tell us that a major canoe manufacturer wanted to speak with us about our trip, and that they may be able to help us out with sponsorship. Robert left with her to go into the town of Terlingua. He spent over an hour on the phone with them to find out they were not going to help out. He spent the rest of the night out on the town and returned the next morning.

Above Rio Grande Village was open valley with picturesque mountains off in the distance. The river was shallow and silty, making travel difficult. We had to sometimes wade as far as a mile without being able to paddle. A lot of it was knee deep sand-gravel mix that filled our boots causing blisters and abrasions on our ankles and feet.

Getting back into canyon terrain, we entered Mariscal Canyon. This canyon was over 1800 feet deep in places. It was awe-inspiring, but also known for heavy drug traffic, putting us on high alert. One evening a Mexican armed with a rifle appeared on a bluff across the river from our camp. He asked something in Spanish, but knowing only a few words of Spanish, we didn't know what he asked.

Robert yelled up at him, "No abla espan-yo!"

The Mexican laughed and waved to several people behind him to come forward. They came down along the bluff with bulging packs  and crossed the river 50 yards downstream.

Behind our camp grew tall river cane. Behind that, Robert and I could hear the men digging a hole. As we began to wonder if we were to be put in it, the illegals re-appeared downstream empty-handed and crossed back over into Mexico. The man with the rifle waved goodbye as they all disappeared over the horizon. The next morning we wasted no time with breakfast and moved on.

Leaving the canyon we entered the "Great Unknown", the open desert terrain between Mariscal Canyon and Santa Elena Canyon that is rarely utilized for recreation. In this section of the Rio we experienced more "silty" valley areas. In the shallow riffles we saw dozens of gar spawning. The channel catfish and gar had a lot more spots on them compared to other places we had been. All the hilltops along the open valley areas that we explored had evidence of Native American activity. Flint chips, as well as, whole artifacts could be found, indicating they made their camps and fashioned flint tools atop the hills. We took a lot of pictures of the cool finds and then left them where we had found them.

With all the horror stories we were told about the border, we expected trouble the whole way, but had had no problems. Most of the people were extremely kind. I was angry that I had not learned more Spanish. Some were kind enough to offer food and water despite their humble living conditions.

> Big Bend is a must see National Park. It is identified as a geological wonder of the world. Geologists flock to the area. The park also offers unique plants & wildlife. Its distinctive beauty was hard to beat.

At Castalon, another BBNP visitors center, we watched children playing in the river as tourist utilized the ferryboat crossing over into the small village of Santa Elena, Mexico. We made camp at Cottonwood Campground. A friend of Robert's had joined us for a visit and took us sightseeing the next day.

We stopped at a restaurant in the re-populated ghost-town of Terlingua, Texas, for lunch and met the owner. He told us that years ago he had been busted for smuggling marijuana into the United States. While in prison, his cousin, Jimmy Carter, gave him a full pardon before the end of his term as President.

Before leaving Cottonwood Campground, Robert and I watched a convoy of government vehicles surround a large RV. The federal agents arrested the people and confiscated the vehicle for drug smuggling.

With just a few miles left of the "Great Unknown", we eventually arrived at the mouth of Santa Elena. It's the most visited canyon of Big Bend NP, and people were everywhere, including Steve. He and his wife, Debbie, were the owners of Rio Grande Adventures. He gave us a couple of hats and told us he would put us to work as guides after completing the expedition.

As we entered the 1200-feet canyon, we spotted several other canoes going upriver. Talking with their guide, Christen, she told us that they were doing a section called the Upriver Santa Elena. The short trip went up two miles to Fern Canyon for lunch and then returned the way they came. Fern Canyon was a large side canyon with several ferns growing from seeping springs that joined Santa Elena from the Mexican side. After exploring it, we made our way up to Rock Slide Rapid.

The Class II-IV rapid, depending on water level, was formed by cabin sized boulders obstructing the river's flow. The smooth water carved boulders laid between sheer 1200-foot limestone walls. The beauty of the dark canyon was humbling. We made camp early and spent the rest of the afternoon soaking up the natural beauty and listening to the call of the canyon wren.

We battled several more rapids as we made our way out of the canyon. As we approached one rapid, a two-foot gar jumped into my lap and fell to the bottom of the boat. I couldn't stop laughing as I fished it out. The river began to disappear more and more every day.

Our next stop was Lajitas, Texas. Approaching the tourist resort town, it seemed like we had stepped back in time. The town's buildings replicated the architecture of the late 1800's. We took a bath in the river and went into town. The buildings looked old from the outside, but inside they were classy and modern. We made several phone calls to let everybody back home know how things were going.

156

At a new campground being constructed we made ourselves at home and waited on Pete McKaskle to show up.

Pete arrived with brand new portage carts for both of us. His fabricated carts, with the help of a friend, were far superior to any on the market in every way. We spent the next few days fishing and relaxing. We were able to explore the area more by road, thanks to Pete giving us the keys to his truck while he went fishing and said, "Have at it."

Taz took us to Terlingua for a night out on the town. We ended up at a bar and grill called LaKiva. The club was partially underground and had a caveman atmosphere. That night was Alter-Ego Night and all the crazy alter-egos were out to play. The majority of people were dressed in costume and dancing to a local live band. We partook in the madness by only drinking a few beers at a table near the dance floor. A Mexican, who could not speak English, kept trying to ask Robert a question. The man was obviously drunk and high, but we didn't think much about it.

I went to the bar for another beer when Robert came walking up and said, "Let's get out of here."

Asking him why, he informed me that the Mexican had just licked him on the arm. That was reason enough for me, so we found Taz and went over to some of her friends' house. After a short visit, we went back to camp.

Before leaving Lajitas, I tried once again to aquire money from people who owed me back home. Every dollar was becoming more precious due to unexpected expenses, but I still had no luck. Out of sight out of mind, I guessed.

Just upriver was a famous movie set. It's been the background for movies like *Streets of Laredo, Up Hill All the Way, Spy Kids II* and several others, as well as, several commercials. There we saw a huge wild pig scare a pair of German bicyclists by threatening to charge them.

Near "the teepees", a familiar roadside picnic area located at the base of "Big Hill" was home to an alligator. Keeping our eyes open for it, a large dust storm began to blow-in forcing us to make camp and take cover. The sky blackened with a fierce cloud of dirt pushed by strong winds. With our canoes anchored down and our tents flattened around us, we had to cover our faces with T-shirts to keep from breathing in air that was thick with dust. The storm quickly passed leaving everything heavily coated with dust and dirt. We spent the remainder of the day cleaning ourselves and gear.

We paddled up through beautiful Colorado Canyon and met a German couple on vacation, camped out on the Texas side. Robert and I camped on the Mexican side of the river to avoid the state fee that the park charged for daily use. We figured if we camped in Mexico, the State Park couldn't charge us for camping. We had climbed 8 miles of river that day.

The next morning, across the river, Robert saw the German man and woman just waking up and getting up out of their tent. The woman took off her bra. Topless, she began scratching her back with her bra in the same manner you would dry your back with a towel. At the same time she said, "Mornin'!"

"Mornin'," Robert replied.

Both camps were simultaneously making breakfast and talking across the river. We said our goodbyes and paddled on.

Chapter 19
Word From Home

L eaving Big Bend State Park, we meandered our way through open desert valley along a large irrigation canal. The canal was built of hand laid stone and was very impressive. It was fed by a tributary called the Rio Concho in Mexico and irrigated fields and ranches in Mexico for miles. This canal was one of the main reasons why the Rio Grande was becoming more shallow each day.

As we approached Presidio, Texas, the river was almost non-existent and heavily polluted. This was as far as we could travel by river. Above Presidio, the Rio Grande, except for the occasional flash flood, was bone dry and overgrown with tamarisk trees.

We drug our canoes up Almito Creek to meet a friend of Pete's who lived nearby. Charlie wasn't home so we made camp in his yard and waited for him to arrive. When he returned home late that night we introduced ourselves and went back to bed.

The next day Pete arrived and we went into Presidio for an authentic Mexican breakfast. Before heading back to Charlie's, I called home to check-in with my family and to tell them we were going to have to portage to the Gila River in New Mexico. My sister answered the phone and I asked to talk to my mom, but my dad answered instead.

I then received the worst news of my life. My little brother Tony had been killed in a drinking and driving accident. My heart was crushed. Speechless, I hung up the phone. I told Pete and Robert what had happened.

Pete said, "I'll get you home."

I called back home and told them I was on the way. We headed back to Charlie's, where we had stored the gear. Pete called home and told his wife that he was driving us to the airport in Midland, Texas.

The drive to the airport was one of the longest five hours of my life. We arrived without showers, filthy, stinking and still wearing our river clothes. The flight home was like being in the twilight zone. We had spent the majority of the last year sleeping on the ground, living in the elements, out of a tent. The next moment, we're flying thirty-thousand feet in the air arriving in Kansas City in just a few hours.

My family met me at the airport and took me home. I wanted to quit right then and there, and stay home to help support my family, but they all urged me to continue on in my brother's name.

For months, I had been trying to get the people who owed me money to pay-up with no results. Word had spread about my brother's death and that I would be home soon. Before our plane had touched down in Kansas City, all my money had been deposited into my bank account.

After a week of mourning, we met back up at the airport and started back to the Rio Grande. The flight back was uneventful and somber. Pete met us at the airport in Midland and gave us both big hugs.

Robert had caught a cold, and the five-hour drive to the Rio Grande was miserable, filled with coughing and nose blowing. By the time we arrived at our boats, he was running a fever, but had no other choice but to prepare for our portage the next morning.

The Rio Grande was now dry. Our next river with water was hundreds of miles across the desert and summer was just around the corner.

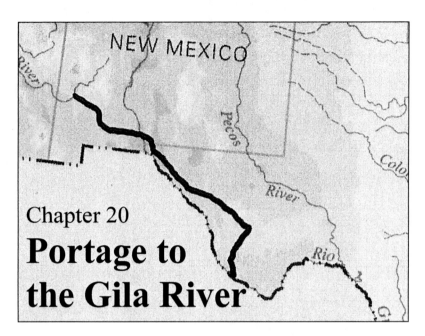

Chapter 20
Portage to the Gila River

April 19 – May 31, 2001

Early the next morning, Robert and I strapped our gear to the new portage carts that Pete built and portaged seven miles into Presidio, Texas. Storms were rolling in and both of us were feeling sick. We purchased a room for the night at a small motel in hopes that a good nights rest would chase away the cold. Waking up the next morning, Robert's condition had gotten worse and I was running a fever. After two more days at the motel, our condition had not improved. Without funds to pay for another night, we had no choice but to continue portaging.

Utilizing the room until check-out, we left Presidio and began the long walk into the desert. We were loaded down with 300 pounds of gear, as well as 6 gallons of water each. We walked the rest of the day, taking breaks every hour or so. Near sunset, after 11 miles of portaging, we made camp under a bridge.

A truck stopped overhead and yelled down to us. We walked up and introduced ourselves. The man and woman had heard about our journey and came down to give us some supper and words of encouragement. After visiting for a while they left.

Sleep didn't come easily that night. Overpasses were commonly used by illegals to hide under, emerging when their transport arrived and we needed to be extra alert.

The next morning we were up early, fixing a pot of coffee. We pulled our canoes up onto the highway, still miserably sick and with sore muscles. By noon, we made it to the ghost town of Shafter. It had many abandoned rock houses with a beautiful spring fed creek. After hanging out for an hour and filling our water jugs, we continued on.

The desert was still in bloom. Roadside ditches were covered with wildflowers. Large prickly-pear cacti were bearing fruit and the ocotillos were covered with bright green leaves. Desert Mountains blanketed with Blue Bonnets, Texas' state flower, towered along both sides of the road offering panoramic views of the remote Chihuahuan Desert.

We were climbing in elevation, leaving the Rio Grande Valley and entering Desert Mountains. Climbing the steep mountain roads would have been taxing just for a man to walk, carrying nothing, let alone pulling 300 pounds of gear and a canoe. We had to lean forward so far that we could touch the ground in front of us. To gain leverage, we would use the cracks in the road in the same manner as a rock-climber would use them to climb a mountain.

Every step was a struggle and we had no choice but to take a break every hundred yards. In order to take a break, the man in back would grab a rock and block the front canoe's tire so the front man could stop. In turn, the man in front would run back to do the same for the guy in back. It was this teamwork that enabled us to traverse what some people refer to as "The Dead Man's Walk."

Summating a mountain hill presented a new challenge. With 300 lbs of gear and a canoe pushing us downhill and no breaks on the canoes, we had to use brute strength to prevent the canoes from running us over. Moving to the side of the canoe, allowing the bow to rest at our hip and leaning backward, we could control the descent. When close to the bottom of the hill, we would pick up the pace and run along side the canoe and ride it out.

After 13 miles of portaging, we had climbed to nearly 5,000 feet above sea level and made camp next to a large boulder locally named Elephant Rock. We were beginning to feel a little better, but were still feverish and ready to stop for the day.

A few miles before reaching a Border Patrol checkpoint, a van stopped and an older couple jumped out. The man had a camera and the woman a notepad and pencil. They walked up and introduced themselves as reporters for a local newspaper called the Desert Candle. We needed a break and enjoyed sharing our story. Robert made them promise to send his parents a copy of the paper and in return promised to keep in touch with them.

Portaging a couple of more miles further, we saw a Border Patrol checkpoint. Approaching the checkpoint, armed men in uniform turned and stared us down as we pulled our canoes up to the stop sign. Several agents circled us asking what we had in the buckets. Robert replied, "A couple of illegal aliens and about 100 pounds of cocaine." The Border Patrol agents laughed and waved us through. We pulled our canoes to the side and took a break in the shade of the Border Patrol building.

After walking another 18 miles, we made it to the town of Marfa, famous for the mysterious "Marfa Lights". It had been 5 days and 60 miles since our last shower and a decent meal. Our feet were throbbing and blistered, and we had developed a nasty, painful rash from our shorts rubbing the inside of our thighs. Purchasing a motel room, we doctored our wounds and enjoyed the comforts of home for the next 12 hours.

Before leaving town the next morning, the manager at Dairy Queen insisted on buying us a meal. After about an hour of conversing with the customers, we pushed on down the road.

As the sun set, we waited until there were no cars in sight, then quickly opened a ranch gate, dragged our gear into a bunch of tall shrubs, shut the gate, and set up camp after pulling our canoes 10 miles that day.

The next morning we pulled our canoes back onto the road and shut the gate behind us. Looking up, we noticed a big white blimp floating in the sky way off in the distance. Robert took out his video camera and zoomed in on it just as a train blew its horn. The engineer stuck his head out and waved to us. We had seen a lot of trains since the journey began and couldn't help but wonder if it was one we had previously encountered.

We continued portaging for a couple more hours and stopped for a break below the blimp we had been curious about. A sign nearby read - *United States Air Force Tethered Aerostat Radar Site.* We watched the blimp land before continuing.

Before we knew it, the sun was setting and we began looking for a place to camp. Once again we slept under a bridge with evidence of illegal alien traffic. There was trash, empty cans of food, graffiti, and well-beaten paths that lead from the desert to the road. All the locals had warned us to be careful and look out for the illegal aliens because they're not to be trusted. Any illegals with a backpack should be avoided at all costs because they're carrying drugs and they won't hesitate to kill.

There weren't any illegals that night, however passing trains kept us awake. We were up at dawn and vowed never to sleep next to a train track again.

We stopped in Valentine and filled our water jugs from a hose behind the Post Office. Late in the afternoon, clouds were rolling in and a big storm was brewing to the south and another one to the north. We came upon a rest area with covered picnic tables and set up our tents under the only shelter we had found for miles. With 21 miles in
168

for the day, we fixed our staple, ramen noodles, for supper as it started to rain.

Robert took out his video camera and recorded an awesome lighting show. We were literally surrounded in all directions by cloud to ground lightening striking all around us. It wasn't just one big storm; it was dozens of small storms with the sun peaking around each cloud, shining down to the ground. The storm continued late into the night.

It was odd to see puddles in the desert as we portaged to the town of Lobo. The only thing that remained was a few deserted homes with graffiti covering the walls. Stopping to take a break, we felt uneasy, as if we were being watched. It was clear no one was living in the homes, but they weren't completely abandoned either. There was an unexplainable gut feeling that evil was in the air, like the calm before a very bad storm. Everything within us said we needed to leave.

After a short rest, we continued down the road and came upon a pecan grove. We wondered why anyone would plant hundreds of pecan trees in the middle of the desert where water is in short supply.

Late in the day and three miles from Van Horn we ran out of water and were quickly running out of energy. We could see the next town, but at our pace, it seemed a very long distance away. When we were about a half mile from a truck stop, light-headed and suffering from heat exhaustion, we got a burst of energy and headed straight for it.

Reaching the truck stop, we parked the canoes, walked in and quenched our thirst. The sun was getting low and all we cared about was finding a room for the night. Robert and I portaged on into town, receiving many strange looks. We found a room for under $20 a night and having spent all our cash on cheeseburgers, I had to walk to an ATM while Robert watched the canoes. I returned with cash about 30 minutes later and we settled in for the night after going 22 miles.

The next morning we woke up sore and exhausted. We didn't think twice about spending another $20 and went back to sleep. We rested and tended to our blisters, rashes and sore muscles before heading toward El Paso.

Pulling our canoes along the shoulder of eastbound traffic on I-10; several cars, 18-wheelers and RVs honked and waved as we crossed paths. When we entered the Mountain Time Zone, we stopped for a break and to absorb the moment. The significance of this location was more than a time change; it was

Top-10 List
Commonly found litter found along America's Highways:

1. Remains of blown-out tires,
2. Beverage Containers: Plastic, Aluminum & Broken Glass,
3. Dirty Diapers,
4. Fast Food Containers,
5. Bungee Cords,
6. Plastic Bottles of urine,
7. Plastic Grocery Bags,
8. Cigarette Butts,
9. CDs,
10. Clothing.

Listed in order by abundance

also the 3,000 mile mark into the journey. Time zones really didn't matter too much since we were living from sunup to sundown. After a long day of walking in the West Texas heat, we sought shelter under a bridge and set up camp.

The next morning was very windy with thick cloud cover. For the first time in months, we were able to tune-in a radio station. The last time we listened to a radio broadcast was in Del Rio, several hundred miles away. It was a sure sign that we were back in civilization even though El Paso was still 100 miles away.

Road construction forced us onto a frontage road. There wasn't much of a shoulder and it was the worst paved road we'd ever seen. It had a 2-inch crack every 50 feet. Each time a car passed we were forced into the ditch to avoid being hit.

During a break, a horse drawn wagon passed by. The last time we had seen a horse drawn carriage was in Missouri where Amish communities were not uncommon. A truck pulled up a moment later and the woman driving asked what we were doing. She explained how a blind man, with the aid of a man with MS, were driving the horse drawn wagon cross-country. They started on the West Coast and were on their way to Washington, DC. They stopped along the way at schools, educating kids about disabilities and how to overcome adversity. She was their support team.

As the sun set, the frontage road came to an end and we waited until there was no traffic in sight, then opened the gate and set up camp. The next morning we were up at dawn and back on the interstate, heading west into eastbound traffic.

A few miles up, we came to a truck stop and pulled in for a break. We ate a quick breakfast and took a few pictures of Tony, a white tiger kept in a cage, as a tourist attraction. A non-profit animal activist group was protesting the facility. Moving on, we approached some more road construction and the interstate narrowed down to two lanes while the old eastbound lane was being replaced. Robert and I stayed on the section under construction and portaged for a total of 18 miles.

The next morning, we checked the air pressure in the portage cart tires. Both carts had slow leaks and with no replacements, we topped them off and continued. We went another 19 miles and camped behind a sand dune along the highway. There was a beautiful sunset that night followed by a good night of sleep.

After another 17 miles of pulling our cumbersome canoes, we finally reached El Paso. The city presented new challenges. The road department stopped and asked us to stay off the freeway, to prevent a wreck. We agreed to use the side roads and go around the heart of the city; a task that would be much easier said, than done.

Walking along, we happened upon the El Paso Museum of History and stopped to gather more information on the area. We discovered that there was no easy way to portage around town and that we must zigzag through the city. The biggest problem was finding a place to sleep. We stopped for lunch and then portaged a couple more miles to a motel. Our funds were low and we really couldn't afford a room, but unwilling to sleep on the streets of El Paso, we splurged and did it anyways.

After carrying our gear into the room, we stood outside to watch a dust storm roll in. A man walked up and introduced himself. He was with the DeWalt Racing Team, and after talking with us for a little while, he insisted on paying for our room. Robert and I spent the evening pouring over our maps, trying to figure the best route through the city.

We stayed on the sidewalks when possible, doing our best to avoid the danger of morning traffic. We walked 9 miles across town dodging brutal traffic and hopping curbs, but were still stuck in the hustle and bustle of El Paso.

Near the International Airport, we got a room. Robert called home to check in and his dad informed him of some substantial withdraws from his checking account. Robert said he had all of his receipts and made arrangements with his father to call the bank.

The next day we stopped in front of Fort Bliss where Robert's dad went to Sergeant Major School. Thinking about his father, reminded him to call home. His dad told him that he was driving down from Kansas City to review the receipts and he had paperwork from the bank for him to sign. He was also bringing our guns and ammo back to us. We filmed a military convoy and paid our respects at the Fort Bliss National Cemetery before continuing.

Arriving at a bridge posted, *No Pedestrians*, we were forced to go underneath it and carry our canoes over some railroad tracks. Just as we made it to the other side, two trains traveling in opposite directions pulled up and stopped, effectively cutting off the way we came. We walked on, hoping we were going the right way.

The clouds started to get dark, and I noticed a tire going flat on Robert's portage cart. However, Robert's attention was fixed on what looked like a tornado in the distance. Being from Kansas, we knew what a tornado looked like. He grabbed his video camera and zoomed in on debris flying around the base. Just as quickly, as it appeared, it disappeared.

After portaging all day, we were in a residential neighborhood, still stuck in El Paso, and the sun was beginning to set. After eating supper, we wondered where we were going to sleep. At a convenience store we thumbed through a phone book and inquired about a place to stay, with no luck.

Just when we were about to give up, a woman walked up and introduced herself. Sandra, a local real estate agent, offered to let us use one of her vacant houses for the night.

Robert called home and discovered that both of our fathers were on their way to El Paso. Arriving the next morning, we got motel rooms, and Robert spent most of the day going through his receipts and bank statements, finding over $700 of fraudulent charges. Thieves had hacked into the bank's computer and stolen money from several customers. The bank refunded the stolen funds after Robert completed the proper paperwork.

We spent the rest of the day shopping for supplies. After breakfast the next morning, our fathers headed back to Kansas. Happy to have seen our dads and to have our guns back, we walked to our canoes and spent the night at Sandra's vacant house.

Sandra greeted us in the morning with a bag of homemade cookies. We said our good-byes and continued portaging down the road. Finally, we made it outside the El Paso city limits and took a moment to celebrate. After three more miles of walking, we crossed the state line into New Mexico. It had taken seven months to travel across the great state of Texas.

We continued on to Highway 404 and headed west into the town of Anthony. Several people had warned us about gang activity in the area. Robert shouldered his shotgun, and I positioned mine within reach as we portaged into town - just in case. However, the gang members that we did encounter just stared and smiled giving us the thumbs-up.

After 24 miles of portaging, we came to a bridge just big enough to hide our canoes under and made camp. It was much easier to sleep in an exposed area with our guns by our sides.

The next stretch of road had no shoulder, forcing us to utilize a very narrow frontage road. We had many close calls with vehicles passing within inches at 55 miles per hour.

At a motel that night, Robert filmed police officers searching the parking lot with a drug dog. Sniffing around the trunk area of a compact car, the dog stopped and lay down indicating that there were drugs present. The policeman rewarded the dog and then returned to his vehicle. Robert and I thought we were going to witness a drug bust, but never saw the outcome.

After three more days of torturous portaging, we arrived at the town of Demming, New Mexico. On the north edge of town a van pulled over and stopped. The man driving invited us to supper and gave us directions to his home. After a good meal, we were invited to set up camp in his yard and use the shower. The next town was Silver City, 52 miles away with nothing but desert in between.

Three days later in the quaint town of Silver City, we were approached by a reporter from the local newspaper. After a thorough interview, we moved on.

Leaving Silver City, there were several miles of 6% grade leading up a steep mountain pass. Climbing the steep switchbacks, we felt every bit of the 350 pound loads pulling back against us.

We finally reached the top of the mountain pass and took a break for lunch next to a sign that read, "Continental Divide Elevation 6230 Feet." With a feeling of great accomplishment, we took a few pictures before continuing down into the Gila River Valley.

Most of the next several miles were downhill delivering us at the banks of the Gila River and the end of our long desert portage. It took five weeks to portage 450 miles, lugging over 350 pounds of gear, enduring fever, bruises, blisters, rashes, sore muscles and traffic using only human power. We celebrated by diving into the river.

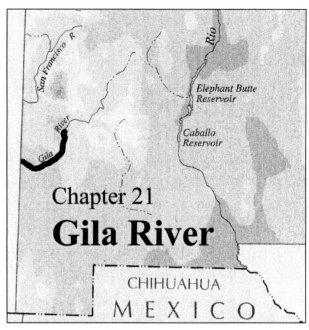

Chapter 21

Gila River

May 31 - June 7, 2001

Birds and butterflies hovered over the clear mountain stream as we weaved our way through a tight granite boulder maze. Sycamore, willow and cottonwood trees lined the river providing shade from the brutal desert sun.

We made camp early our first day below a bluff, on a nice gravel bar. With plenty of daylight left, I climbed up the bluff to do some exploring. The trailblazing was difficult due to loose gravel and rock. The last stretch before reaching the top could only be done by intense rock climbing. Nervously shaking upon reaching the top, I was left breathless by the beautiful view overlooking the Gila. The only manmade thing in view was a mineshaft just across the river from our camp.

Spotting some mountain lion tracks on a game trail, I followed them down the trail knowing that animals always know the easiest route to water. The trail passed by a pine tree growing out of a crack in the side of a boulder. The tree was small, but had an ancient appearance. I sat down a moment to admire it and wondered how many people would have the chance to see it.

A huge lizard popped out from behind the tree. Both of us were startled, and it seemed as interested in me as I was of it. With caution, it moved closer to investigate me. From only a foot away, it studied me for several minutes before darting away to the safety of some rocks.

Moving down the game trail, I made my way back to camp. Next to my tent was a bird's nest with a baby bird in it. I moved my tent down the gravel bar so I wouldn't disturb the mama and baby. Darkness came over us while bats filled the sky collecting bugs. The sky was clear and we enjoyed a star filled night.

Robert took video the next morning of the mama bird collecting insects, then returning to the nest to feed the baby bird. We forged the river armed with flashlights and cameras to explore the mineshaft. On the way we spotted fresh bear tracks that indicated a bear had passed within only 50 meters of camp the night before. Cautiously we approached the mineshaft that was partially covered with tumbleweeds. We pulled away the brush and entered the shaft to discover it only went in a short distance and stopped.

We returned to camp, packed up, and moved on down the rapid infested river. Not far, we came upon a group of pack mulers who were doing some backcountry fishing. We talked for a while telling them of the bear tracks we had found. The group had also seen some bear tracks and showed us a large stringer of catfish they had caught. The pack mule guides warned us of dangerous rapids in the Lower Box Canyon only a few miles ahead. They also told us about a destroyed and abandoned kayak in the canyon.

The granite walls closed in tighter as we made our way downstream, giving us even larger, more dangerous rapids to maneuver through. We found the kayak the group had told us about, not far into the canyon. It was broken nearly in half and left for dead. From the looks of it, whoever owned it may have been hurt badly and had to walk out.

Scouting was impossible for a large part of the section, so portaging wasn't even an option. In one very technical rapid, my shorter canoe could barely be turned through the boulder maze. So when Robert, in his slightly longer canoe reached it, he got pinned and dumped. He nearly wrapped his canoe around the boulder, but somehow with all his strength, he prevented it by pulling the swamped canoe back upstream against the swift current. Saving his gear could have killed him, but he knew his gear was his lifeline this deep in the wilderness.

Seeing that Robert was in trouble, I slung the front of my canoe up on a boulder to hold it in place and ran back upstream, hopping boulder to boulder to help.

Robert yelled, "I got the boat. Grab my gear!" I tossed the floating gear up on a tiny gravel bar as Robert freed the canoe. Then Robert yelled, "My video camera!"

I reached down in the water and it rolled right into my hands. I set it on a nearby boulder and we searched the swift river bottom for anything else that was salvageable. Everything else we wrote off as missing in action. As we continued down, we fished floating gear out of the eddies.

The canyons disappeared behind us as we paddled into an open valley. The rapids turned to riffles separated by deep clear pools of water. Looking down into these pools, we could see schools of trout, catfish, and carp. The valley began to show signs of agriculture with the presence of cattle in and along the river. We then paddled through another short canyon, seeing birds of prey and a flock of bighorn sheep.

Just outside the canyon, the river was dammed and disappeared into a man-made tunnel flowing underground through a mountain. Scouting on foot, in what should have been the riverbed, we found the location where the water was being diverted. From the underground tunnel, irrigation canals dispersed the water in many directions. Farmer's had pirated 100% of the river.

Walking some distance further, we came upon some houses where we met "Farmer John". He informed us that he used to own all the surrounding area. We asked if there was any water downstream, but he had no information. I asked how it could be lawful for one person to take the whole river. He then turned hostile, screaming, "Them damn Indians down river are also complaining about water rights and are suing the landowners upriver."

"I would be angry too if someone stole the river out of my backyard," I responded.

The situation was beginning to escalate, so we walked away leaving him mumbling. The guy was being unreasonable and we weren't going to waste any more of our time on him.

Walking back to our gear, we noticed leaks in the old irrigation canal. The water was naturally returning to the dry riverbed. After portaging down the semi-dry riverbed a couple of miles, we finally had enough water to float the canoes and walked while pulling them behind. Contaminated excess irrigation runoff was also flowing into the riverbed providing more water to float our canoes.

Not only did the farmers take the whole river, they were also pumping large amounts of ground water into the irrigation canals dropping the aquifer 150 feet or more in only a few years. We passed several more diversion dams and thanked God, they leaked, too.

After three days of torturous conditions, we arrived in Duncan, Arizona. We walked two blocks from the river to a local tavern. The locals told us the river only got worse, and they were surprised that Robert and I had made it this far down the dried up river.

Dreading another long portage, we sat down and got drunk while debating whether or not to continue. In the days of Lewis & Clark, expedition leaders would give the men small amounts of spirits each evening. Thus, when the spirits ran out and because they were so far away - it was too late to turn around. We had passed the point of no return long ago and after some spirits, we decided to continue. The remainder of the day was spent cleaning gear and packing up for another long portage.

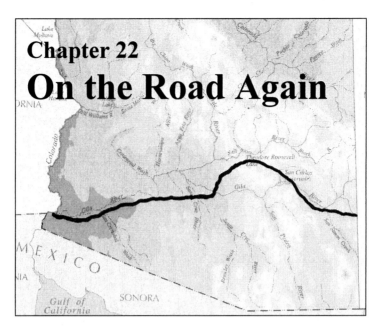

Chapter 22
On the Road Again

May 31 – July 9, 2001

W ith our canoes fully loaded and back on our carts, we left the river and portaged our canoes on up the mountain and out of the Gila River Valley. We expected to paddle the Gila River to the California State Line, but now faced a portage over 500 miles through the Sonora Desert in the middle of summer. The thoughts of quitting were pushed aside as we walked west on Hwy 70 with canoes in tow.

Forty miles away we arrived in the town of Safford. A reporter from the Eastern Arizona Courier asked for an interview and took us out for lunch at a local Chinese restaurant. During the interview Robert and I gorged ourselves from a bountiful buffet. After the meal, we posed for a few photographs before pushing on.

We portaged until sunset the next day and set up camp just out of view along the highway. Nearly asleep, I noticed strange noises coming from a set of bee boxes a short distance from camp. Standing up and looking around, I spotted a large black bear trying to break open the boxes for the sweet honey inside. I yelled over to Robert, "We've got movement!" and the bear franticly sprinted off into the thick creosote brush, making a huge commotion.

By the time Robert was able to climb out of his tent the bear was long gone. We found it strange to see a bear out in the middle of the desert and figured it must have come down from the nearby mountains looking for food.

Robert and I knew we must get through the desert as fast as possible, or we were going to die. We had discussed the idea of using bicycles to tow our canoes and cover more mileage faster, but had never seen it done before. In Geronimo, Arizona we came to a convenience store that had used mountain bikes for sale - priced from only $25 each. Robert bought one to experiment with the idea. If it worked, I would purchase another one.

Robert took his paddle and duct taped the blade to the bow of the canoe and then tied the tee handle under the back of the bike seat. He jumped on the bike and peddled the whole rig around the parking lot making a big circle. We couldn't believe how smooth and easy it was. Before Robert finished his lap around the parking lot, I was already heading inside to buy myself a bike. With both of us now using mountain bikes to pull our canoes, we had a much better chance of getting through the desert alive. Daily temperatures were now exceeding 100 degrees and the level of urgency to get through the desert could not be higher.

We peddled down the road and stopped just outside of San Carlos Indian Reservation to take a break. A carload of Apache stopped and introduced themselves. They invited us to camp in their yard, but with plenty of daylight left, we decided to make more miles.

The bikes had proven to be very effective for traveling along the flats and for downhill. The bikes also provided much needed brakes and less wear on our bodies to control the descent. However, we were still forced to push our rigs uphill. After twenty-eight miles in for the day, we were feeling very fatigued.

We were still in the heart of the Reservation with the sun setting and were becoming desperate for a place to camp. Stopping at a gas station to fill our water jugs, we learned that it was Native American Independence Day. A couple of young men suggested that we could camp under a bridge just down the road. The manner in which they described the place seemed like we were being led into an ambush. We thanked them for the information, but had no intent on following their advice.

Shortly after the young men walked away, an older woman walked out of the grocery store. Spotting us, she stopped dead in her tracks, looking completely dumfounded. She seemed half panicked as she told us, "You don't belong here! You better come camp in my yard." When we asked about camping under the bridge, she said, "Oh no! They killed a man a couple weeks ago down there."

I was suffering miserably from muscle cramps and her offer could not have come at a better time. We followed her to her house that was only three blocks away. We pulled our canoes into the fenced yard and Robert quickly set up and got in his tent. I, like most nights in the desert, chose to sleep out with the stars.

That night, off in the distance, we could here the reservation's Independence Day party celebration. There was live music in between the talking of guest speakers. When a song finished, the crowd would explode into Indian war cries. The sounds were very intimidating and we were very happy to be in the safety of our host's yard.

Up with the sun, I discovered that I had acquired sleeping buddies in the night. Several dirty, flee-ridden puppies had curled up next to me to keep warm. We packed up and peddled on after thanking our host. Several people stopped and offered water; one man even gave us a watermelon. Climbing several steep mountain passes, we successfully made it to the western edge of the reservation reaching the town of Globe.

Navigating our way through the busy city streets, Robert wiped out when one the portage cart tires slipped off the sidewalk flipping his canoe over, spilling his belongs into the street. Robert quickly grabbed the watermelon that was rolling down the road into traffic. I helped flip the canoe back over and gather up the gear so we could let oncoming traffic move on.

Looking up, we were right in front of a motel. We hauled our canoes over to the office and got a room. Just as we opened the door to our room, the phone rang. I answered it hearing, "What the heck are you doing?" A DJ from a local radio station had heard about a couple of guys pulling canoes thru town and had to find out what the story was. After a short version of the story, the DJ asked if he could "put me on the air". I gave my consent, hung up and told Robert what had happened.

The next day we continued portaging and were cheered on by several people who honked and waved as we peddled past. Before leaving town we stopped at a local retail store to re-supply. While I was waiting outside for Robert to finish shopping, a construction worker handed me a $20 bill, "for the cause."

Down the street, we stopped at a grocery store for more supplies. A lady, who was waiting for her husband outside, had a tree branch with a small nest attached to it. Within the nest was a tiny baby humming bird. She found the nest on the ground with the baby bird beside it and was attempting to rescue it. We took pictures of the baby bird and continued on.

Leaving Globe, we climbed several miles of 6% grade forcing us to take many breaks. Eleven miles out of town we found a nice flat spot about 50 yards off the road and set up camp. About an hour after dark I heard several people moving around the perimeter of our camp. Stepping out of my tent I could see the silhouette of a man on the horizon. "May I help you? May I help you! Robert, you better get out here!"

Robert grabbed his shotgun and jumped out of his tent. I explained how I had seen people walking around our camp and thought we were being surrounded. Robert asked if I was sure, thinking it was just a bear or something. "Damn sure! Look up there!"

Robert looked up and saw the same silhouette standing about 30 feet away. He yelled out, "Hey! We have guns and I will shoot!" The silhouette immediately disappeared, leaving us with a sinking feeling that something bad was about to happen. We agreed to take to the bushes and wait for the aggressors to come into camp. I guarded one side, Robert the other.

After about an hour of complete silence, Robert yelled, "Screw this! I've had enough. Either I'm getting shot or I'm going to shoot someone. I ain't waiting in the bushes no more." I yelled out, "Come on!" We decided to be hunter instead of the hunted and searched the bushes around camp.

We needed to get the police involved, if we were going to get any sleep and started walking toward the highway. When we reached the highway, we found an empty van that was not there before. Robert yelled, "We got your van!" A car drove by and Robert tried to wave it down. With a shotgun in one hand and a flashlight in the other, he persistently tried to wave down every car that passed, but no one would stop.

Finally a carload of older men stopped to see what was going on. We explained our situation, and one of the men called the local sheriff. Two officers showed up and ran the tags on the van discovering it was stolen. We all then took to the bushes looking for the van's occupants. After a thorough search of the area, we found evidence suggesting that they were illegal aliens and long gone. The van had gotten a flat tire next to our camp coincidently.

We apologized to the officers for calling them out there over some illegal aliens. One of the deputy sheriffs told a story about how he had been attacked by a car load of them only a week before. The officers left and we finally were able to go to sleep around 2 am.

Despite very little sleep, we were up early and peddling the steep mountain highway. The road had no shoulder making the passing traffic extremely dangerous.

Reaching the summit of a high mountain pass, we took a break at a roadside park called "The Top of the World." Appropriately named, the rest area offered a breathtaking panoramic view of the Tonto National Forest valleys below. The higher altitude also provided us with a much needed break from the extreme temperature. At the hottest part of the day it only reached the mid-90's.

Robert took down a fence and we pulled our canoes through to a shady spot to spend the rest of the day. Shade trees, wildlife, beautiful scenery, and a nice cool breeze made it the best place to camp we had seen for quite some time. We passed the afternoon working on our portage carts, eating the watermelon and hiking.

In order to beat the heat, we got an early start. The first few miles consisted of 7% grade making it difficult to slow the heavy loads. The road did level out some, but continued on a downward slope making the miles nearly effortless. Moving at a much faster pace, we passed through a narrow tunnel with ease.

Robert started to lose his brakes during the final approach to Superior, Arizona, so we released our brakes and coasted - reaching speeds of 20 to 30 miles per hour. We came to a stop at a local convenience store parking lot after traveling over 10 miles in less than an hour.

Douglas Chadwick, the writer we met on the Rio Grande River, had made contact with us requesting we sign releases so he could mention us in his new book. While we were stopped, Robert used the pay phone to call Doug and thank him for including us in his book. After he got off the phone, we stood around talking for a while with the locals posing for a few pictures before continuing on.

The next few days we averaged over 25 miles a day in the 100+ degree heat. The bikes were making the miles pass faster than expected, but it was still far from easy. Blisters and rashes were healing in some places, but regretfully showing up in others.

Early in the morning, south of Phoenix, Arizonia, Robert contacted Darrell. He was one of the cyclists we had met on the Missouri River traveling with the *Face of America* team, and he had told us to call when passing through. After a brief phone call, we made arrangements to meet that evening around 5 o'clock.

About a mile from our destination, a tire on Robert's portage cart started leaking. We quickened our pace, and made it to the truck stop as the tire went flat. We made arrangements with the owner of the truck stop to store our canoes there while we went into Phoenix. With hours to spare, we ate a late lunch and packed the bags we would take with us.

Darrel showed up right on schedule and we loaded up and drove into town. A half-hour later we pulled up in front of a very nice home located in the suburbs of South Phoenix. We cleaned up and Darrell took us out to eat. Back at the house, we took a late night swim in his pool.

The next day Darrel left to give a motivational speech at a local hospital about his life, living in a wheelchair. He said to make ourselves at home and we spent the day relaxing by the pool and watching movies.

That night we went out to eat with Penny, a reporter for the Arizona Republican. After an hour and a half interview, Darrell took us to a micro-brewery where a group of his female friends were waiting for us. Darrell introduced us to Stephanie and several other girls and we hung-out until midnight.

Darrell was moving the next day and we had agreed to help pack and move him. Early morning, the portable storage container arrived. Robert and I began filling it, while Darrel ran a few errands around town. After twelve hours of working in temperatures over 100 degrees, we didn't feel like we were getting much "R&R".

Darrell had made arrangements with Stephanie to put us up for the night. Robert and I went over to her house where she had beds made up for us. We had agreed to help out a friend of hers, who also needed some help moving. The three of us talked for about an hour, but being exhausted, we all soon turned in for the night. Darrel showed up later that night and dropped off $80 each, for the day's labor. He was on his way to the airport for a conference in New York.

We woke early the next day and Stephanie fixed us coffee and called her friend Rose. She was still packing everything into boxes and would call back when she was ready to move. We were able to take advantage of the free time by going to the store and purchasing supplies needed for portage cart tire repairs.

We went over to Rose's apartment and began carrying boxes down to the garage. Her parents brought sandwiches over for lunch. After finishing with the boxes, Rose gave Robert a bike. His bike was near death and the timing could not have been better. He thanked her and loaded it into the truck before we drove back to Stephanie's house. That evening we grilled steaks and hung out by the pool.

We woke-up early the next morning and Stephanie fixed breakfast and introduced Brian. He had arrived late that night and slept in his van. He had been with her husband, Brett, on an expedition sailing around the world. Brian explained how the hurricane season had stopped them in the Caribbean, and he flew home for a couple of months. Brett was securing storage for his sailboat and would be home in a couple of days.

Brian offered to give us a ride back to our canoes. We loaded his van with our gear and were about to leave; however, after he started the van we discovered something was wrong with the motor. It was obvious the carburetor was fouling and Brian said he would get a ride to buy a new carburetor.

Somewhat knowledgeable in automotive repair, I suggested that we take the old carburetor off to see if we could fix it first. I found a missing screw, replaced it and we put the carburetor back together. Starting it up, the engine was running smoother but needed more modification. After a couple of more adjustments the van was purring like a kitten. Brian was very happy that he didn't have to buy a new carburetor.

The repairs had taken all morning. Brian said if it was okay with Stephanie, he would buy groceries to cookout and we could relax by the pool one more day before leaving. Everyone agreed, so Brian and I went for supplies. Rose came over with a friend, and it was turning into a party. Soon after Rose arrived, Stephanie's mom showed up as well.

Stephanie's mom said she had seen two people in Texas doing the same thing, pulling canoes down the road. She said it was a guy and a girl though. After more talk it turned out she had seen us in Texas and had confused Robert's long blonde hair as being a woman's. Everybody at the party had a good laugh over it. The festivities lasted late into the night.

We all woke the next morning and gathered in the kitchen for coffee. After McDonald's for breakfast, Robert and I said goodbye to everyone and headed back to our canoes at the truck stop. Brian dropped us off and began his long drive home. The photographer from the Arizona Republican arrived and took a couple of pictures while we tied our bikes to the canoes, fixed flat tires and then loaded our canoes with gear. After two hours with the reporters, the temperature was already 110 degrees.

After the reporters left, we walked across the street to a closed motel. We found the owner and explained all we needed was to get out of the heat. He opened a room for us and only charged $30. There was no TV, but it was air-conditioned.

On the move before sunrise, we were able to peddle most of the way arriving in Gila Bend by 11:30. We rented a cheap motel room for the night trying to escape the 120 degree temperatures. It was so hot outside the air conditioner had problems keeping the room below 90 degrees.

The next day was Independence Day, so we decided to stay another night and spent the day relaxing by the pool. That evening we turned on the TV and watched several Fourth of July specials. An hour after sunset, just across the street, the local fireworks display began. I watched the display, relaxing by the pool.

After five miserable days portaging through the desert, covering 116 miles, we arrived in Yuma, Arizona. A city block away from the California border checkpoint, we spotted a gas station billboard stating: "Last chance for low prices. Stop here for gas, groceries, and cheap…" We stopped for last minute supplies and continued on to the checkpoint. The officer checked to make sure the canoes had no

produce, plants or other contraband before waving us through the gates. Crossing the Colorado River, we entered California and made camp along the river bank.

Chapter 23

Southern California

July 9 – October 20, 2001

Robert and I stopped at the first gas station we came across the next day to fill our water jugs. The owner informed us we would have to pay 50 cents a gallon to fill our jugs out of the water hose. No one anywhere throughout the entire journey had charged us for water out of a hose.

The store owner's explanation was that he had to compensate for the cost of drilling the well. This was an expense we had never dreamed of. Resentfully, we paid for the water that was necessary for survival.

Down the road near Imperial Valley Lake, we met Jim and Gina who invited us to their lake home for the night. We went for a swim and took showers before sitting down to a home cooked meal. Early the next morning we continued portaging west on I-8.

Daily temperatures exceeded 115 degrees and the extreme heat was taking its toll on both of us. Suffering the symptoms of heat exhaustion and near death, we entered the city limits of Ocotillo, California. A man on an ATV rode up and introduced himself as Jim. He gave us something cold to drink and said we could get out of the sun at his place.

Jim insisted we make ourselves at home and left. Later he returned with a sack full of alcohol. We repeatedly turned down his offers to drink with him. The last thing our stressed bodies needed was alcohol. Before the afternoon was over, the whiskey turned him into a raging lunatic. Sitting on his couch playing a guitar, he would pause occasionally and scream at the top of his lungs towards us, "I rule! You suck!"

The more he drank the more delusional he became. We would have gladly continued down the road had we not been sick from heat exhaustion. We made camp in the shade near Jim's house and did our best to recuperate from the stress we had put our bodies through.

After dark, in a drunken rage, Jim walked into camp and started screaming, "What's my dogs' names?" Standing over me, he leaned forward and again screamed, "What's my dogs' names!"

I believed the drunken madman was actually going to attack me and drew my gun that lay beside me. Looking down the barrel of my shotgun, he mumbled, "Oh, you got a gun. I ain't scared." He then stumbled away and went inside taunting us from a distance.

We decided it would be best to leave as soon as possible and departed at first light.

We had been crossing Imperial Valley for days. Several people warned us about how the area was heavily used by drug runners crossing into the U.S. and that some of those people could be dangerous. The Border Patrol was finding dead bodies out in the desert and the cause of death was not always heat related.

Evidence of illegals was scattered across the desert. Water jugs and empty Mexican food wrappers were present under every bridge. Several places we discovered where cars had been set fire. Criminals used the burning vehicles as a distraction against law enforcement to smuggle contraband and people just down the road. After the sun set the desert was busy with activity. Several times we were awakened to illegal immigrants passing through our camp.

Imperial Valley is located in the southeast corner of California. Water from the All American Canal has transformed the below sea level desert into one of the world's most productive agricultural areas. At the bottom of the valley is the Salton Sea, which rests at 235 feet below sea level. The valley also holds the Algodones Dunes, one of the largest sand dune fields in the country. The valley's mild winter temperatures and a variety of recreational activities make Imperial Valley a popular winter destination.

Outside of Ocotillo, California, we had made the mistake of camping in a rendezvous location. Just before sunrise we awoke with dozens of people speaking Spanish around us. Within minutes a passenger van flipped their headlights off and pulled to the side of the road. The large group fought their way into the van trying not to be left behind. As the van sped away, one of the passengers repeatedly screamed out in despair, "Where's Ricky?"

Reaching the western edge of Imperial Valley, we started up the side of a steep mountain. Climbing seven miles of 6% grade, we made camp under a highway overpass. Late that night a Border Patrol helicopter spotlighted us for several minutes mistaking us for illegals.

The next morning we finished climbing the 16-mile hill - summating into a much cooler environment. From the other side we had a view that continued for miles. With Robert in the lead, we took advantage of gravity and rolled off the mountain. I was traveling at a minimum speed of 20 miles per hour, but still watched Robert pull away. Not using any breaks, he reached speeds exceeding 45 miles per hour. At that speed with the load he had, one mistake would have probably put him out of commission for a while. Several miles later I caught up to Robert, who was smiling ear to ear.

Our spirits were high again. Just being out of the 120-degree heat of Imperial Valley gave us reason to celebrate; we had survived the desert. We stopped in Live Oak Spring where we met a man who needed some laborers for two weeks work. After several hours he never returned to pick us up.

Not far from Live Oak Spring, we stopped at Cleveland National Park, a trail head for the Pacific Crest Trail. I hiked several miles up the trail and had to literally force myself to turn around and head back to the canoe.

We stopped in Pine Valley, home to world-class bicycle training grounds. We

> The Pacific Crest Trail spans 2,650 miles, from Canada to Mexico, passing through California, Oregon and Washington. The trail leads hikers over diverse terrains, traversing; desert, glaciers and volcanic peaks to name just a few.

met the #1 ranked American cyclist at the time, Trent. He gave us some much-needed bicycle supplies and turned us on to some of the finest mountain biking trails in the U.S. I spent the afternoon riding trails and then returned to camp.

Near the edge of San Diego, we took a couple of days off at Lake Jennings to get rested up and try fixing Robert's bike. The bike's free wheel mechanism had locked up causing the pedals to turn at the same pace as the wheels. Rolling down hills, the pedals would turn wildly out of control. To prevent the metal pedals from cutting him up, Robert kept his feet off the pedals as he coasted down the hills.

Making our way through the busy streets of San Diego, the anticipation of seeing the Pacific Ocean itched at our weary souls. Riding all day, we crested the final hill, receiving our first glimpse of water. A short distance further we arrived at Mission Beach, looking out over the horizon of the Pacific. Robert and I looked at each other, nodded and shook hands. We had survived the "Southwest Passage."

Next to where we stood was a hostel, and the manager told us we could stay for the night, except we would have to leave our gear outside. After coming so far, we didn't want to take the chance of being robbed.

Outside we ran into a police officer that was searching some teenagers for contraband. When he was finished, we asked him where we might find a good place to camp. After listening to our story, the cop informed us it was against the law to camp on the beach. He finished with, "Heck, you've come this far. You just do what you gotta do."

The hostel manager's jaw dropped as he turned to his friends and with a surfer's accent, "Dude! That cop just told them to break the law, man! That's the coolest thing I've ever seen, dude!"

We ended up at Campland that night. The tent sites were little more than a patch of dirt packed so tight it was like sleeping on concrete for $27 a night. We stayed there another two days to fabricate spray skirts for our canoes before tackling the ocean.

That night a bachelorette party moved into the site next to us. The three women were drunk and shortly after setting up their tent, they grabbed a young man walking by and dragged him into the tent. He screamed, "No! No!" as they stripped him of his clothes. The poor guy suddenly sprinted out of the tent putting on his clothes as the girls started laughing. Robert and I joined the party; however, two of the girls started chanting over an Ouigi board as the bachelorette began puking. So we returned to our camp to avoid inevitable trouble.

Back on the beach, we attempted to launch our boats into the ocean in order to test the spray skirts we had made. The surf was too high, forcing us to portage to a sheltered cove in La Jolla, a popular launch area for boaters, a couple of miles up the coast. We met some other paddlers who claimed to know the guys who held the record for the longest canoe journey. They wished us luck and in turn, Robert gave them his bike as a souvenir.

Breaking through the surf, we made our way onto the open seas of the Pacific Ocean. Paddling across the surface of huge swells, we found ourselves fighting strong coastal currents that prevented us from making good mileage. Late in the day, we spotted a beach with few people on it, which was rare for Southern California. We decided to try and land there to make camp for the night.

Timing the waves, I dropped-in to the breaking surf paddling as hard as I could. Catching a good wave, I surfed the canoe right up onto the beach without taking on any water. Robert also surfed in, but did so with a boat full of water. Surfing the canoes gave us a huge adrenaline rush. At that moment, I truly understood why surfers were so enthusiastic about their sport.

The shore we had landed on was Blacks Beach, and we quickly discovered the reason for it being nearly deserted - the beach was clothing optional. An older, naked man approached us and tried to start a conversation. It was the first time either of us had been propositioned by a naked man and it did not take him long to figure

 out we didn't swing that way. Eventually, he continued down the beach after a few uncomfortable minutes of conversing.

The next morning we broke through the surf and only took on a little water. Escaping the crowds of Southern California, we paddled atop the huge swells again, both exhilarated by the experience. After paddling several miles, we crash-landed on South Carlsbad State Beach, where we made camp at the park's Hike and Bike. If you hiked or biked in, it was only a dollar to camp.

While there, we met Joe, a 75-year-old man who basically lived off the back of his bike. Joe showed off some of his amazing artwork, while we cleaned saltwater off our gear and shared adventure stories.

The next morning, Robert attempted to paddle out past the breaks, but his spray skirt failed, filling the boat full of water. The next wave spun his craft around leaving him sitting in his canoe completely filled with water, just below the surface. Attempting to paddle back to the beach, the large waves threw him on shore.

Soon after, I tried and made it through five crashing waves, when I spotted a huge rogue wave. Looking straight up at the monster as it began to break, my 15 foot canoe was stood up on end and flipped right over on top of me. Robert and over 100 spectators in unison gasped, "Oh!" from the beach and bluff above.

With my pride crushed, I swam my boat back to shore through the crashing surf. Back on the beach, a small crowd of vacationers surrounded me to see if I was okay. They all agreed it was the best wipe out they had ever seen.

After that, we emptied our canoes to dry out our gear and waited for the surf to die down. The surf only got larger the longer we waited. I did some body surfing to pass the time and finally we gave up, packed our gear and went back up the steep beach access to make camp.

The next day, with the surf still high, we portaged eight miles to Oceanside. We put our canoes in at Oceanside Harbor and paddled nine miles against terrible headwinds and strong currents. That day we paddled past Camp Pendleton where Robert completed Marine Corps boot camp. Several of the Marines doing maneuvers aboard amphibious assault vehicles gave us the thumbs-up.

Reaching the boundary of the Marine base, we made our move to go ashore. The surf was up, and we crash-landed with neither form, nor grace. Robert was flipped forward end over end, being crushed repeatedly in between the canoe and the beach. He finally freed himself, and with little injuries, dragged his gear ashore and started bailing out the canoe.

I was not as fortunate. A large wave threw my boat sideways shifting the gear and pinning my left foot in the canoe. The next crashing wave then ripped me from the boat tearing a large gash across my Achilles tendon. As blood spurted out, all I could imagine was a shark taking the rest of my foot off.

I grabbed the bowline of the canoe and swam towards shore. The injury was so painful I couldn't swim, using my left leg. Reaching shore I crawled up on the beach exhausted and in terrible pain. Even though Robert was injured too, he sprinted over to help.

We had landed on yet another clothing optional beach. Moral was low as we discussed how these waves were small in comparison to what was ahead. We were bummed-out, taking a moment to regroup. I cleaned my wound and wrapped it up before we made camp.

Just before dark a huge military hovercraft landed on the beach within 75 yards of camp. Two soldiers emerged from a hatch and lit a cigarette. I grabbed my camera and snapped some pictures. The hovercraft suddenly came to life becoming airborne in an instant. As quick as it came in, it disappeared on the horizon.

The very next morning the surf was even bigger. Frustrated with battling the surf, we took out our maps looking for a river. The closest navigable river was the Salinas, and even better, it was flowing north, parallel to the coast. The first challenge would be getting off the beach. Trapped between a two-hundred-foot bluff and impenetrable surf, we had no choice but to portage up the beach to a trailhead.

The gash on my foot was crusted over and infected causing severe swelling. With our gear loaded on the portage carts we pushed on. The sandy beach caused the carts' tires to sink into the loose sand. Three feet at a time, we would pull, then take up the slack and pull again. Progress up the beach was slow, making for a brutal portage.

After a quarter mile of this; Ed, a lifeguard, drove up in a truck and asked if we needed any help. After a short conversation, he offered the use of the showers located at the lifeguard headquarters before driving away.

After two miles of torturous portaging through crowds of naked people, we arrived at a trailhead. By now my foot was causing me so much pain it had become a serious concern. I cleaned out the wound with the remaining freshwater we had left, before climbing up a very steep dirt trail to get to the lifeguard headquarters.

About halfway up, Robert came back down the trail to help me up the steepest section. I was at the front pulling the bowline with Robert pushing from behind. The bowline snapped and suddenly all 350+ pounds of canoe and gear were pushing against Robert. Loose gravel below his feet gave way as he began to slide off the high cliff. In fear for Robert's life, I shouted, "Let it go!" Inches from the edge Robert got a foothold and I grabbed the bow of the boat. If not for Robert, I would have lost everything over the edge of the hundred foot cliff. We fought gravity the rest of the way up and took a well needed rest.

As we limped along the bicycle trail towards the lifeguard headquarters, half-serious and half-joking, I cursed Robert for not letting my boat and gear crash to the bottom of the cliff. "You're not getting out of this that easy." Robert insisted.

Eventually we made it to our destination. As we approached the headquarters, we felt like we had just walked onto the set of *Baywatch.*

Looking in the mirror at tattered clothes, long hair, scraggly beards, and peeling sunburns, we could see why people thought we were vagrants. After a shower, shave, and a clean change of clothes, we were given a tour of the headquarters. Ed and some of the other lifeguards took us out to eat at a fine Mexican restaurant.

We stayed in San Clemente for a few days to allow time for my injury to heal. Leaving town, a reporter followed along to take pictures of us portaging. The pictures were later published in an article he wrote for the Sun Post News.

At Doheny State Park, we made camp early because of my foot. Tobie, a young man we had met in San Clemente, stopped by with supplies to barbecue hamburgers and started cooking. His sister's boyfriend walked up intoxicated and set a six pack of beer in the back of the truck. The young punk-rock kid was acting like a fool, drawing attention from others using the beach. He talked loudly about hating cops and then began relieving himself in the bushes rather than using the restroom located nearby.

Minutes later two park rangers came out of the bushes, grabbed both of them and forced them to the ground. Tobie began resisting the officers, forcing them to use more drastic means for restraining him. Screaming in pain, he asked what he had done wrong. The officer responded by telling him he was in possession of alcohol on a state beach. The kid's father was contacted to pick him up and he slapped him as he tossed the kid in the car. After an hour had passed, they gave Tobie a warning and escorted him out of the park.

An older woman with a group nearby asked if it was drugs. I told her the charge was possession of alcohol and she went back to her group to hide their contraband.

The next morning we woke up to maintenance personnel cleaning the bathhouse next to our site. Using a hose, they rinsed urine and toilet paper from the bathhouse right into our camp only inches from our tents.

Leaving Doheny, we spotted a small creek dumping into the ocean along the beach's edge. Just the smell of it made me want to puke, not to mention what was in it. At the creek was a sign stating, "Warning! Contaminated water. Urban runoff/storm drain water may cause illness. Avoid contact with ponded or flowing runoff and the area where runoff enters the ocean." We found these signs common along the coast of Southern California and could see why people were getting hepatitis from swimming in the ocean. This sign though was unique. On the same signpost was a sign stating, "Marine Life Refuge".

Just past the creek was a harbor. We walked down to the boat ramp and prepared to launch the canoes, all the while sharing conversation with a man who worked there. With everything packed and ready to paddle, the man told us it would be $10 each to use the boat ramp. With no money to spare we began setting up to portage again.

A passerby named Steve, whom we had met earlier in the day, started to cuss the guy, saying, "You no good s.o.b.! These guys are doing something amazing dude and they shouldn't have to pay." It was the man's place of business and Robert and I weren't going to argue with him. Without saying a word, we finished packing and portaged on down the road.

All but a handful of people we met since entering Southern California were rude and inconsiderate of anyone around them. Not only were the people less than tolerable, it was the most polluted place we had ever been. All this and we still had to portage through Los Angeles and then some.

After 441 days of expedition, stress was taking its toll. As we walked along Huntington Beach, a large group of drunken college guys began yelling obscenities from a third story balcony. I snapped, yelling back, "You want to run your mouth, come down here and say it to my face!" Robert had my back and followed it up with the same.

An extremely large man, part of their group, of at least 300 pounds looked down at us with disbelief. Looking back and forth between Robert and I, and their group, he yelled over to his friends, "Shut up in there!," followed up with a nod of respect towards us.

Robert and I finished by saying, "That's what we thought, can't back up your mouth." and moved on.

We were completely disgusted with Southern California and pondered the question that everyone asked: Why are we doing this? Having accomplished more than anyone had ever thought we could, we told ourselves we could quit any time, with no shame. We were stressed beyond our limits, low on cash and tired of each other. The respect we had for each other was equaled by how much we loathed the other. The main factor keeping us going through this stretch was that neither would quit first.

On the north edge of Huntington Beach, the crowds diminished and we took a break near some surfers who were barbecuing. The smell of the cooking meat was torturous. The only guy in the group asked if we wanted a burger. Without hesitation, we simultaneously said, "Yep," and joined the group.

Brett was the surfer's name. We sat with them and talked, mostly about surfing. After a tasty supper, we said goodbye and walked down the beach to find a place to camp.

For miles, signs all along the beach stated "No Camping", so we were forced to walk on into the night. Hours after sunset we found a pay parking lot in front of a Coast Guard office. Exhausted we pulled into one of the parking spots and put some change into the meter. After snacking on some treats from Brett, we got some sleep. The next day was going to be brutal; we were on the edge of Long Beach.

Long Beach was gridlock, forcing us to use sidewalks for much of the day. We constantly had to keep an eye on our gear. Several people just reached into our boats grabbing what they could. Gang and drug activity was prevalent everywhere we looked. Several people stopped in their tracks at the sight of us. Some gave warnings like, "Don't use side streets," and "Don't stop here for the night." We were way ahead of them on that already and pushed hard through the madness of Long Beach.

Stopping at a rough looking convenience store, we bought a couple of cold sodas and took a break. We briefly explained ourselves to a few curious people, but most of them walked away thinking we were just vagrants. A police officer was trying to pull through the parking lot and with all the traffic; my canoe was partially blocking the path.

Robert screamed at me to move it out of the way. I didn't like his tone, and before long we were in a shouting match and about to fight. People gathered, watching us before we finally called a truce and moved on.

After 19 miles of walking for the day and no place in sight to camp, we stopped in Harbor City and found a cheap rundown motel to stay in. Up and down the street as far as we could see were strip clubs and porn shops. There was no choice but to leave our canoes outside in a carport, out of the room's view. So fed up with how things were going, we shut the door and hoped the boats would be stolen.

"Damn it! They're still here," we both said the next morning. We loaded up, strapped ourselves to the canoes and walked on. Portaging all day in heavy traffic along the Pacific Coast Highway, we had many close calls. Things improved a little as we passed Hermosa

Beach. People were still offensive and laughing at us, but they weren't being as rude.

Stopping on the boardwalk for lunch, a man invited us to his beach house for a cold drink. A few minutes later we arrived at his house where several other people were gathered. He introduced himself as Brad, the former publisher of Hot Rod magazine. His wife brought Robert and me a cold drink and we all sat around the patio table talking.

A few neighbors stopped in and asked what the story was with the canoes. Several of them thought we were lying. A neighbor named Brett invited us to his place, a couple of houses away. After moving everything to Brett's yard, Brad and Brett fed us a huge meal of Chinese food and pizza. After supper we camped in Brett's yard.

The next morning, Brad gave Robert a mountain bike. It was one of the best timed gifts of the expedition. The bike was nearly new, top of the line and badly needed. Our spirits were high as we tethered the canoes to the back of our bikes. We could now make better mileage, getting us to the Salinas River quicker.

Not far we arrived at the famous Venice Beach. The bike paths were packed, making it difficult to navigate our 26-foot long rigs. A woman on roller blades started cussing Robert for taking up so much of the path. She wasn't looking where she was going and did a face plant in the grass lining the path.

It was impossible for us to stay together. Robert was ahead about 50 feet when a man from the crowd shouted, "Run away canoe!" I looked up and saw the crowd part as Robert's canoe barreled through.

Robert quickly stopped his bike and grabbed the canoe moving it off the path. The paddle that joined his bike and canoe had snapped under the tension. We repaired it quickly and moved on. Venice Beach was known for being a freak show and we thought we might blend in with the crowd. To no avail, we still drew a lot of attention. Even street performers pointed and stared.

Finally through the most crowded sections of Southern California, the next thirty miles of Highway 1 passed along the edge of the Santa Monica Mountains National Recreation Area. The road coursed a parallel route along a less populated area, offering breath taking views of the rugged shoreline.

Pulling our canoes through Ventura, we spotted a major outdoor apparel distributor and stopped to inquire about sponsorship. The employees we talked to were intrigued by our story, but the upper management refused to take time to talk to us. We left and continued portaging to Carpinteria State Beach and camped in the Hike and Bike section.

The highway traversed inland away from the coast leading us over an area of open hillsides known as the California wine country. Utilizing a small country back road, we were free of traffic and made camp next to a clear mountain stream. Being free of light pollution that night, we were given our first clear view of the stars in weeks.

We portaged to Santa Maria the next day and found a Wal-Mart. We took a break while shopping for some much-needed supplies. A TV crew showed up and interviewed us. The reporter said it would air that evening, but we were unable to see it.

Several days later, after long painful miles of portaging, we arrived at the Salinas River below Robert's Reservoir. The small clear stream was used to irrigate thousands of acres of fields growing produce and grapes; thus, offering plenty of water to float a canoe.

Waking up after our first night on the river, we threw more wood on the fire and started coffee. While eating breakfast and listening to the radio, three deer walked out into the river in front of camp, only 30 feet away. They seemed to not even notice they were being watched as they played and splashed in the water. After about 15 minutes they looked up and acted surprised to see us. They then bounded off into the woods as if it were life or death.

The small stream flowed through rural countryside passing through several vineyards. Free from civilization, we finally felt like we were on a canoeing expedition instead of a bike ride. Several days later we arrived at Gonzales and camped under a bridge to await some family that was coming to visit.

Early the next morning a construction worker working on the bridge above us asked if we had heard what was going on. Confused by his question, he simply stated, "Turn on your radio" and walked away. It was the morning of September 11, 2001. Miles from town, our only link to the outside world was a small radio. We sat under the bridge listening to mixed reports of desperate announcers repeating over and over that the United States was under attack.

The World Trade Center and Pentagon were hit, airlines were shut down, and Robert and I were stuck in the middle of nowhere. As far as we knew the whole country was under attack. We rode our bikes into town and called home to talk with family. On our way back to the river, we spent the rest of our money on food and ammo.

We moved our camp downstream to the next sand bar and continued listening to the radio. People were angry and feeling patriotic. We were now 4,359 miles into the journey, and unsure of what was going to happen. For the time being, Robert and I decided that the best place to be was on the river. It was a scary time for us.

In the wine country, in order to protect the vineyards from birds, the farmers use propane powered noise makers. Approximately every 20 seconds or so, the noise makers produce a loud blast like gunfire. The only activity in the skies came from fighter jets doing maneuvers. The sounds were unnerving.

The next morning we awoke and had coffee. Most of our waking moments were being spent listening to news reports. Rescue efforts were still going on in New York City. At that time, they estimated 4,700 dead. The whole nation, including Robert and I, was angry and scared.

My Aunts Helen and Karen showed up and we moved our camp over to the Laguna Camping and Race Grounds after chaining our canoes to a utility pole under the bridge. My aunts took us to area tourist attractions, as well as, Big Sur. There we were able to explore some trails under the canopy of large coastal redwoods.

After a nice visit with my family, we returned to the river to find that our canoes had been stolen. The remainder of our belongings that were left behind were spread about 50 feet around, leading away from the scene of the crime. Asking the foreman running the bridge construction if he had seen anyone take the canoes, he said he might know where the canoes were. Instantly, Robert and I knew who the culprit was, even though he wasn't admitting guilt. The foreman said he could probably get them back by morning and did so with the exception of one portage cart.

I explained that the cart was just as important as the canoe, but the guy was still being difficult. He kept promising over and over that we would get the rest of our gear back. Furious, Robert got in the guy's face and said, "There are two kinds of people - talkers and doers, and all I see is your lips moving. We're calling the cops!" The man started to say something and then walked away.

We called the sheriff and assured that we wouldn't press charges if everything was returned. After talking with the foreman, the deputy sheriff said if the gear wasn't back in three hours, to call him back. Three-and-a-half hours passed and we headed to town. On the way, we were flagged down and presented with the rest of our gear. The only excuse the foreman gave was that he thought we had gone back to Kansas, never to return. He never admitted to taking the canoes, and he didn't apologize.

Chapter 24
Parting Ways

After 9/11, the water feeding the river had been shut off at the dam leaving us no choice but to portage. In between us and the San Joaquin River was the San Juan Grade. The road was steep offering little to no shoulder. Despite the difficulties, the scenery was beautiful.

Overlooking an open valley, ground squirrels barked between one another below. Occasionally we saw eagles and hawks swooping down, trying to attack the squirrels. We commented on how the people driving by at 60mph probably never got the chance to see nature at work like we were. From the top of the pass was a fantastic view over looking vineyards in the distance.

Pacheco Pass was very difficult to climb, and with it behind us, we thought we were home free. However, the down side of the pass created more problems than the rest of the portage. The shoulder was very narrow to start with, but the real problems were warning track and large rocks that had fallen from the bluffs above. With the gravity of a 6% grade pushing us, we had to dodge rocks, traffic and warning track at 15 to 20 miles per hour. Several times we had to bring the 400 pound loads to a complete stop in order to prevent being smashed by semi-trucks rolling down the mountain.

Before reaching the bottom of the mountain pass, my front tire blew out and the paddle connecting the canoe and bike broke. Reaching back with one hand I grabbed the bow of the canoe and

brought everything to a complete stop and made repairs.

At San Luis Reservoir we stopped for a break, and to see if the rangers would watch our gear while visiting with some of Robert's family. The rangers informed us that they could not and would not watch the gear. So, not far down the road we found a RV resort that was happy to accommodate. Robert called his cousin Sam and we went with her into the city of Fresno.

After spending some time with Sam, we moved over to Robert's Aunt Jo's house for a few days. While there, she took us to Yosemite National Park for a day of sight seeing. It was cool to spend some time in one of America's most beautiful National Parks. After a nice visit, we were taken back to where our gear was stored.

The next day we pushed hard and arrived at the San Joaquin River. Wasting no time, we launched the canoes and paddled downstream. We could physically see salmon in the waters below, migrating to their birthplace to spawn. A lot of people were on and along the river, some looking suspicious.

While passing a fairly popular recreation area, we were paddling side by side talking when all of a sudden, shots rang out from behind a thick bunch of cattails that lined the bank. One of the bullets was only a couple of feet ahead, while the other went right between our heads. The shooter was only 20 feet away, perpendicular to our position. It seemed like everything was in slow motion. I could actually see the percussion of the bullets pass by us.

I yelled out, "Hey!" and instantly we heard footsteps run a short distance and stop. We wanted to shoot back, but were afraid of hitting someone innocent. Dropping our guns, we paddled hard to put some space between us and the shooter. There was no doubt the shooter knew we were there. Putting a bullet two feet from someone's head was not a practical joke, and it definitely wasn't an accidental discharge. We believed there was divine intervention.

A couple of days later, we met a blonde woman fishing along the river. Robert and the girl hit it off, so we set up camp and hung out for a while. While there, the radio announced that the river was closed just downstream because of a large fish kill. Later that evening, a friend of the blonde girl showed up and we all sat around the fire drinking.

The next day Robert and the two women went to town for more food and supplies. Robert sat up front with the blonde, and her friend sat behind him. Looking in the side mirror, he saw that the other woman was holding a knife and giving him a psycho look, like she planned to use it on him.

"Hey, what are you doing?" Robert asked.

The blonde looked back, yelled, "No!" and slammed on the brakes, bringing the car to a complete stop. The slim figured blonde wrestled her large framed friend from the car, leaving her standing along the highway. It turned out, the other woman was the blonde's girlfriend, and she didn't like the way Robert was looking at her girl.

Robert and the blonde continued into town and picked up the supplies we needed. On their way back to the river, they saw the other woman walking down the middle of the highway into speeding traffic.

A couple of days later we heard that the river was reopened and we moved on. Just down river, we paddled into an environmental disaster. Salmon, shad, bass and darters were among the tens of thousands of dead fish floating on the surface. The three suspects of the cause were: a water treatment plant, agricultural pesticides and a dairy farm.

The revolting smell stripped us of any positive attitude we had left. To add to the misery, the entire valley had a stench to it already. The smell partially came from the yellow haze that covered the valley. In every direction away from the river we saw commercial farms spraying their fields with chemicals.

Paddling among the dead fish, a crop-dusting plane swooped down and sprayed us with a cloud of chemicals. Our exposed skin began to burn as we covered our faces with our t-shirts to prevent breathing the fumes directly. We wanted nothing more than to be away from the most polluted river valley we had ever experienced. It was getting dark as we made it through the main part of the fish kill, and we made camp on an island infested with mosquitoes.

The next day, we both woke up in bad moods. The smell of the dead fish passing by with the current sickened us to the point we could not eat breakfast. Paddling on, I put space between myself and Robert. It wasn't long before we were far out of sight of each other. Our planned route was to turn left upon reaching the delta, but I chose to go right instead, paddling into the town of Stockton.

Robert arrived at the Delta and continued on our original course. Not having the map, he still had a general idea of the direction that he needed to go. After several miles of paddling, he stopped at the first convenient spot available for camping and waited. A few minutes later, I paddled over to where Robert had landed. Robert waded out into the water, grabbed my canoe and yelled, "Where have you been?"

The first words to come out of my mouth were, "That's it. I've had enough. I'm going home."

At that moment we both knew we needed a break from each other. I gave Robert the map and some cheeseburgers I had bought for him in Stockton, and pushed my canoe back into the water and paddled off toward the Sacramento River. It was official, we were parting ways.

Chapter 25

My Solo Begins

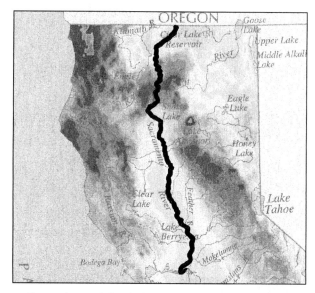

October 20, 2001 – May 4, 2002

The first night alone, I camped along the outer edge of a private pheasant hunt-camp. All night, pheasants could be heard clucking, which made me homesick. (I was born in the pheasant capital of Kansas.) The next morning I decided to paddle on for two more weeks. Wherever I was at that point would become my wintering spot.

It was late fall and the mosquitoes were at their thickest for the year. I traversed out of the delta area utilizing the Mokelume River into the Georgiana Slough and then onto the Sacramento River. The lower Sacramento River was completely channeled by steep, man-made rock shores. Highways ran parallel along the banks making it difficult to find privacy to relive my bladder. After paddling a few miles without seeing a spot to set up camp, I paddled back down to the Georgiana Slough.

Over three hundred miles of the river lay ahead of me as I restarted my ascent of the Sac. Near the delta, the current was almost non-existent, making for an easy paddle. Hundreds of fishermen were on the river looking for a fight from the large migrating salmon. This river was much healthier than the San Joaquin, but still showed signs of pollution.

Fighting the current north for two days, I could see the high rise buildings of the state capitol city on the horizon. The section of river that flowed through the city of Sacramento was very congested with boaters and fishermen. Showing no river etiquette, very few waved and no one took responsibility for their wake.

Making it to the north side of Sacramento, I found a rare sandbar and made camp early. All day fighter jets had been flying low and fast in the area, when out of nowhere, a huge antique float plane landed and took off right in front of me. It was an awesome sight to see on such a narrow river.

Storms and wind were very common ascending the Sacramento. Nearly everyday I was greeted with a strong headwind. The current continually pushed harder and harder with every mile.

One evening two otters approached me and began to get very aggressive. Within 5 feet of my tent, one of them barked and splashed until I ran it off. The next morning, only 50 feet upriver, I found a young dead otter. Poking it with a stick, the body was still limp, but showed no obvious signs for the cause of death. I took GPS coordinates and a photo, then moved on another 50 feet and spotted a beaver. Stumbling out of its den, it appeared to be sick and disoriented. Moving very slowly, it stumbled into the water and swatted the surface with almost no power. It swam off like a dying fish disappearing into the depths. I reported my findings to a wildlife research team I met upstream.

Two weeks after parting ways with Robert, I secured my gear in a storage unit in the town of Colusa and took a bus home for the winter. While home, I visited my brother's resting place and spent time with my family and friends. I also talked with Robert and we agreed that we would continue the journey together when our paths crossed sometime down the road. Obtaining employment, I was able to secure funds for financing the continuation of the expedition.

My parents dropped me off in Colusa, mid-March 2002. I packed up and portaged two miles from the storage facility back to the river.

After several hugs and good-byes, my parents started the long drive back to Kansas.

The river was much higher than I had last seen it. It was clear, cold and moving fast against me. Paddling was not always possible. Those times, I would wade—sometimes chest deep—fighting the fast cold water.

A few days had passed and I realized how much I had needed the break from the expedition. Despite rough conditions, I was having a good time again. Waterfowl, osprey, beaver, otter, deer, salmon and turtles were among the wildlife I saw along the river. The river valley was also home to many orchards that were in full bloom. Off in the distance, snow still covered the mountains.

About 200 miles upstream, the river bottom changed from gravel to river carved stones. The channel also narrowed, creating an even swifter current. My feet were constantly cold, wet and bleeding. Looking at my battered feet, I remembered a girl back on the Rio Grande who asked, "Why are you wearing boots? Like, how are you going to get your feet tan?"

My answer was, "Because I would like to keep my feet." I changed footwear from sandals to boots and felt dumb for not doing it sooner.

Some sections were so swift that I would wade 20 feet along the edge, pull the canoe up to me by its bowline, then wade and pull again; repeating the motions until clearing the rapid. I considered it a victory to climb 10 miles of river in a day.

Finally reaching Red Bluff, California, the river changed again. Red Bluff to Redding was probably my favorite section, but the toughest to ascend. Getting closer to the mountains, the water was significantly colder, but made for good trout fishing. Guided drift boats passed daily as guests fly-fished for rainbow trout.

While camping at Red Bluff, I saw some teenagers smashing swallows in their nests under the bridge. I yelled at them, watched them pick up more rocks and do it again. After threatening them with violence, they ran off. It made me furious to see anyone unnecessarily kill an animal that eats mosquitoes.

Above Red Bluff, the river ran through volcanic canyon terrain. Entering the canyon on the west side of the river, I saw a submerged aluminum fishing boat that some unfortunate soul had lost. I tried to free the vessel, but could not overcome the powerful current of the river that was holding it in place.

Just around the corner, on the same side of the river, I discovered an interesting sight. In the middle of the river was a huge flat-topped boulder, which was barely submerged below the surface. From the top face of the boulder, shot a small water fountain. Further investigation revealed the water was being funneled thru the massive boulder and immerging pressurized from a naturally formed hole in the rock.

Moving upstream between the steep walls of igneous rock, I discovered China Rapids, a narrow two-mile section of swift water. The water was bone chilling cold and deep with wicked boils that could easily flip a canoe. Even motor boats feared the place, due to several boats being lost each year there. Half way up through the maze, a jet boat came through and asked if I was okay. After confirming I was, they shook their heads and moved on.

The rugged volcanic terrain was beautiful, but made for difficult travel. Exhausted and hungry, I made camp on the first gravel bar above the rapids. It was the longest set of rapids I had ever climbed. At camp I watched several passing fishermen catch and release trout.

The Sacramento proved to be a challenge to climb, forcing me to cross from bank to bank to paddle in calmer waters. One particular riffle, when paddling across to the eddy side of the river, the current was so swift that I was swept downstream 200 yards. Even fighting the current, my GPS recorded that I had traveled 15 mph backwards. It was the fastest I had ever traveled in the canoe, too bad it was in the wrong direction. Upon making it to Redding, the mountains were close and I knew another portage was only a few miles away.

After another night on the river, I portaged several miles over steep hills into Redding making camp at the Redding RV Park. It was an opportunity to heal blistered feet and to allow Robert to catch up. I met Jack and Carol, the owners of the park. After doing laundry and cleaning up, Jack drove me almost to the Oregon State line to scout my portage route. Knowing what lay ahead, relieved a lot of pressure from me.

Jack and Carol were the nicest and most helpful people I met in the entire state of California. After saying goodbye, I continued portaging around two dams and launched my canoe onto beautiful Shasta Lake.

Shasta was full of water for the first time in years. The large lake was surrounded by tree covered mountains, accented by Mount Shasta. It was not hard to see why the lake was designated as the houseboat capital of America. Most of the marinas rented them, and there were hundreds to choose from. The lake had so many coves; a person could have one to themselves, even on a busy weekend. Back in one of the secluded coves, I had a black bear wander through my camp one night.

One of my pieces of gear was a Walkman that had all the options including TV and weather band. Handheld weather radios rarely worked making the TV band very helpful in obtaining news and weather reports. One day listening to the news, a reporter came over the air waves talking about somebody paddling up the Sacramento River. Having no doubt who it was, Robert's voice came over the air. He was near Chico, CA, at Scotty's Landing. I paddled over to Lakehead Marina and called down there. Robert was still there and we had a chance to talk to each other, instead of just relaying messages through our parents. I informed him I was on Shasta Lake and ready to portage north. Robert was still two weeks behind and insisted that I go on without him.

The highway along the rapids of the upper Sacramento River, had a good shoulder for portaging, but I battled constant tire and bike problems. I had the bike purchased for $25 in Arizona, tuned up in Redding at a local bike shop. The service cost me $62 and they insisted the bike would make it several hundred more miles, it made it 11. Tearing the bike apart along the roadside, I figured out the problem and fixed it myself.

A couple of days later, a deputy sheriff stopped me and asked to see my identification. Asking the officer why he stopped me, he answered that he wanted to check me for warrants, inferring that I could be on the run from the law. I told him that pulling a canoe up the side of a highway was no way to hide from the law.

While the officer ran my ID, a Cal-Trans truck pulled up. In it were Kurt and Tom, two road workers. They asked if the cop was harassing me, and I responded, "Yes" as the officer handed back my ID and turned to leave. Kurt, Tom and I sat along the highway's edge talking awhile. Kurt then offered me supper at his house just up the road.

Before getting there I had to climb a 5,100-foot pass. Prior to reaching the summit, my bike basically fell to pieces and a tire on my portage cart blew. I fixed the flat tire and walked on. Completely exhausted, I finally limped into the Cal-Trans depot around dark. Kurt lived in the employee housing next to the workshop.

After a shower and a hot meal, Kurt and his wife drove me to a Wal-Mart an hour away to buy the cheapest bike I could afford. Kurt also helped repair some of my gear back at the shop. He helped me more than anyone could ask of a stranger. That night I camped next to Grass Lake, located next to the Cal-Trans property.

The following day I summated Mt. Heron Pass (5,202 feet) and talked to Tom at a turnout near the summit. Coming down the other side of the mountain was a blast. For about five miles I flew down the 6% grade at 30 miles per hour. Down below was a flat valley as far as the eye could see. After riding for several hours into a strong headwind, I made camp only 13 miles from the Oregon State line.

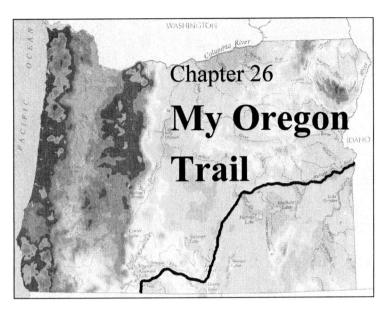

Chapter 26
My Oregon Trail

May 4 – June 7, 2002

On May 4, 2002, I crossed into Oregon. The first several miles were labeled a National Wildlife Refuge but all I saw were irrigation canals and farms. Portaging around Klamath Falls, to avoid city traffic, Highway 140's shoulder ran out leaving me fully exposed to traffic. After nearly being run over several times, I turned around and went back to town. The map I had was specifically designed for bicyclist. It showed that Hwy 140 had a four-foot shoulder, but the map was completely wrong.

Back in Klamath Falls, I searched for better maps, but couldn't find one anywhere. Even worse, nobody would talk to me; it was like a bad dream. After a couple of hours of searching for info, I had nearly crossed the city of Klamath Falls. Only a few blocks away from a bike shop, a large burly man walked up and complimented me on my portage cart. The man's name was Roger and he invited me into his house where he had several topographic maps of the area. He told me of a rails-to-trails path that followed Hwy 140 for about 60 miles. He warned that most of the trail was dirt and gravel; also, that he had not traveled much of the trail.

Roger and his wife invited me to stay the night and have supper. Over the evening, I learned that he was a forest firefighter and in his down time traveled and worked in fur trader reenactments. At the shows, he displayed artwork created from his blacksmith and canvas skills. Roger also informed me that he lead sermons on Sunday mornings. They were a great couple and I regretted not being able to share more time with them.

The trail leaving Klamath Falls was paved the first few miles making for smooth travel. Four miles out of town, the trail was nearly unused and mostly composed of loose gravel. Unable to ride, I unhitched the bike and strapped myself to the front of the canoe like a mule. Looking over at the highway and seeing no shoulder, I was happy to have the trail that was preventing me from being run over.

The nights were still cold, usually in the 20's, making it difficult each morning to leave my warm sleeping bag. Daytime temperatures were perfect, typically in the 70's. Even though the calendar claimed it was late spring, it snowed until noon twice along the 63-mile trail. The snow posed no navigational threat since it melted as it hit the ground.

The trail became more difficult each day as it led me into the higher elevations of the mountains before me. What posed the most hindrance was the loose volcanic gravel covering the trail. The tires on my portage cart sunk into the loose lava rock creating so much resistance that I actually had to forcefully pull my canoe downhill to make any progress. The loose gravel also made it difficult to get traction while climbing over the steep mountain passes, which were brutal.

Fifty miles into the trail, after an early start, something was approaching from behind. Looking back, I saw a large piece of machinery that appeared to be a steamroller. Upon closer inspection, I learned that it was a steamroller that acted like a jackhammer, packing the trail as it went. The man on it stopped and introduced himself as Art, the president of the local rails-to-trails organization. He informed me that he packed the trail every spring. Had I known that, I would have waited a week.

Noticing the poor condition of my bike's back rim, he and his wife Maureen, drove out that evening and straightened the bent wheel. Both were cross-country bicyclists and had a few stories of their own. They were not the only visitors that evening. Bill, with

River Spring Ranch, brought me fresh meat and a 6 pack of tall boys. It felt good having company.

From start to finish, the trail took me through 63 miles of beautiful Oregon landscape, consisting of tree topped mountains with marsh grass valleys. The trail ended in Bly, Oregon, where I was able to re-supply at a local grocery store. I learned at the National Forest Headquarters that the backcountry road I planned to use was closed due to snow covering the road. The road would not reopen for at least another month.

Left with three options, I pondered; wait a month, take the mountainous Hwy 140 with no shoulder and heavy truck traffic or take a ride. With more than 5,000 miles human powered and only enough money to get home; I knew I couldn't break the record this attempt and that I had nothing to prove. What I really wanted was to get home alive.

I took a ride and was glad I did. The highway was extremely dangerous. Several places along the road, there was only a foot of shoulder beyond the white line before dropping over a cliff. Along the way, I saw semi-trucks taking up the entire lane. If I had pressed on, I probably would have been hit, or caused a wreck from somebody trying to avoid me.

Forty-three miles later my ride dropped me off in Lakeview. Walking along an outer road, I stopped to photograph and video a geyser that erupted about every 30 seconds. Continuing up Hwy 395, a reporter from the Klamath Falls newspaper stopped to interview me.

About 30 miles north, I stopped in Valley Falls. The only thing there was a gas station and convenience store. Dave, the owner, told me that if I was looking for the middle of nowhere, I had found it. Looking at my rig, Dave asked if he could give it a try. After riding around the parking lot, he remarked, "Better you than me. That's hard work!" Dave warned that the next services were over 80 miles away, so I topped off my water jugs before moving on.

The highway presented no problems with traffic, even with no shoulder; the road was nearly abandoned. There was sometimes a 20 to 30 minute break between vehicles. The road soon began to follow along the shoreline of Lake Abert.

The huge blue lake was beautiful, but salty. To avoid only one day's worth of paddling and salty gear on the other side, I decided to continue my portage. It was so salty; the only thing able to live in it was brine shrimp. Bordering along the road was a very picturesque 2,000-foot bluff caused by a fault line that stretched for miles.

The next few days I made great mileage despite cold rain and snow. Several people stopped to talk, telling me they had seen me in the Klamath Falls newspaper. Many of them gave me snack foods and sodas.

Several miles northeast of Wagontire, Oregon, I was awakened by the sound of hoofs trampling the ground near my camp. Stepping out of my tent, I was surprised to see a herd of wild horses gathered only 50 feet away. After a few moments of staring each other down, the herd galloped away, disappearing over the horizon.

Eventually I made it to Riley at the junction of Hwy 395 and 20. My portage cart tires were bald to the point that the threads were showing. My last spare was basically useless; it had a huge bubble in it and a hole where the tube was exposed. Looking up, I saw a billboard that stated, "Only 25 miles to new tires."

After climbing two miles uphill past the sign, one of the tires on my cart blew. I used duct tape to "re-tread" the worthless spare and sat it aside. Knowing that only a miracle would get me the next 23 miles, I hoped for a ride in order to get a new tire. After two hours of trying to hitchhike, nobody stopped to help. Putting the lumpy spare on, I was able to coast back to Riley. Just as I arrived in town, my spare blew out. Dale and Pat, at the Riley Store & Archery, let me camp out while I went looking for a tire.

Waking up the next morning, I "re-treaded" the lumpy tire with more duct tape and put it on so I could at least move my rig around. A nice couple offered me a ride to Burns, which was the closest town that could possibly have had a tire. Taking them up on their offer, I loaded my gear into their pickup. They dropped me off at the local tire franchise, but they didn't have the size tire I needed. They did offer some other places to check, so I began my search riding down the street on the "re-treaded" tire.

A thin, tall man on a three-wheeler stopped to talk to me. Jim, a local mechanic, took me into his house where he called every store in town that might have some tires. None of them had any in stock; but he assured me not to worry, he had friends that might be able to help. We drove all over town visiting Jim's friends and finally ended up with three slightly-used tires for only $25. To order just one, would have cost more than that. Thanks to Jim, I was road-ready again, with two spares.

Memorial Weekend was about to begin and Jim insisted that I stay with him and his family to avoid the holiday traffic. Jim had me lock up my gear in his garage to go with them into the mountains for the weekend. We loaded up several motorcycles and drove a couple of hours to a beautiful camp up in the mountains. Jim's neighbors were already there, and we joined them around the fire. Our camp was surrounded by tall ponderosa pines with a small, clear mountain stream cutting along side. We rode for hours, exploring the gravel roads that fingered throughout the National Forest.

Only a few miles from camp were the ruins of an old mining community. Not long ago, it had been home to over 3000 people infected with Gold Fever. Several old buildings were still there, but most of them were in a dilapidated state. Tin cans and other debris, left behind by the miners, littered the area surrounding the buildings. We visited several of the mineshafts, but entered none because of the hazardous conditions found within. Most of the vertical shafts were filled with water. Some antique heavy equipment was there as well. It was fun to explore some of America's past.

Back at camp, we panned for gold in the small mountain stream, but only found a few flakes. At the end of the weekend, we came off the mountain to find that traffic was still heavy.

Before leaving, Jim took me over to meet Emory, a friend of his. Emory and his dad were obsidian rock experts. From the volcanic rock, they made beautiful Indian artwork. He and his dad made the finest obsidian pieces I had ever seen. Emory showed me the step by step process of working raw obsidian into a useful piece of artwork. They knew enough about the field that archeologists from the Northwest would go to them for information about their finds. Emory also gave me some insight into the Native American history of the Northwest.

While giving me a lesson of the area, he chipped out a five-inch spearhead and gave it to me as a gift to remember him by. It was a truly educational experience. For the first time, I was thankful for my tire problems. If I hadn't needed new tires, I may have never met Jim and his friends.

Leaving Burns, the road was brutal heading west on Hwy 20. Climbing steep pass after steep pass, left my feet blistered and bruised. It was early June, but the weather was still frigid in the mountains. One day, I found myself caught in a torrential downpour, with the temperature only around 40 degrees. I was completely soaked in the wind driven rain, and began to go into hypothermia. My skin turned blue as I was shivering to the point of convulsion.

Knowing I had to do something or die, I set up my tent. Before getting the rain fly on, a large pool of water had collected in the bottom of the tent. Grabbing all the cotton clothes I had, I sopped up the water and threw them out onto the ground. I then stripped out of my wet clothes in the pouring rain and dove into the tent. Drying off the best I could, I then put on every piece of dry winter clothing I owned.

As warmth began to return to me, it gave a burning sensation. Once I was able to move my hands without severe pain, I cooked and ate a hot meal. Eventually my body returned to normal and reality set in. The fact that I had almost died again weighed heavily on my mind.

Taking the next day off and looking at the map, I saw it was only 32 miles to the next river. Pushing hard the next day, I crossed over two mountain passes and reached that river.

Launching my canoe onto the rapid infested Malhuer River, I made great time paddling down the clear, fast mountain stream. The tall mountains that towered above were 10 different shades of pastel, making for a beautiful landscape to paddle through. However, there was also constant boulder dodging and barbed wire fences to navigate, making it not so ideal for canoeing.

Several times I would not see the barbed wire fences until the last minute. To prevent disaster, I was forced to jump out of the canoe into the swift rapids and stop the canoe. I would then forge the river to the safest river bank, and lift the fence in order to slide the canoe under. After about 15 miles, the river calmed and turned its course away from the highway, back into a hidden valley.

The hidden valley was an opportunity to camp away from the highway noise. An hour after making camp, a rancher approached me asking what I was doing on his private property. Stepping out of my tent to explain, a coiled up rattlesnake struck at me. So there I was, trapped between a heavily armed rancher questioning me and a rattler two feet away from my bare feet. I yelled, "Rattler!" and grabbed my shotgun, pointing it at the snake. The rancher yelled across the river, "Don't just sit there. Kill it!"

I shot the coiled up snake and the rancher looked pleased. I explained that I only wanted to stay the night and would leave first thing in the morning. The rancher gave me permission to stay and then told me to get off the river a few miles down. He warned the river went into a diversion tunnel that pirated most of the water. Disappointed to be leaving the river, I would be on the road again until reaching the Snake River.

For the next two days, the highway offered no shoulder and heavy traffic buzzed me on a continuous basis, I was happy to be launching my canoe onto the Snake River at Nyssa, OR. The river marked the state line, giving me reason to celebrate. There was only one more state to pass through before reaching the continental divide. From there, all flowing waters would lead me home.

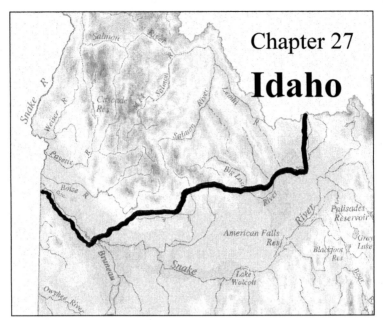

Chapter 27

Idaho

June 7 – 27, 2002

Climbing several miles of the swift Snake River offered constant view of wildlife. Turkey, quail, deer and lots of waterfowl lined the river. The river was shallow and had many islands that were great for habitat, but bad for navigation. I studied my maps because it was already mid-June and to follow the river would cost me valuable time. The plan was to meet up with Robert somewhere on the Missouri River and follow the Lewis and Clark trail home before winter arrived. Reluctantly I got back on the highway that ran semi-parallel to the river.

Back on the highway, I became ill. Most of the drinking water in the Snake River Valley tasted like sulfur, which only added to my suffering. I wasn't drinking enough water and was unable to keep food down for several days. Weak and malnourished one mile outside of Murphy, Idaho, I collapsed into a roadside ditch in the 100-degree heat. Lying in my own vomit for several hours in the desert heat, nobody stopped to help.

Finally a pastor and his wife stopped and gave me fresh cold water, which quickly made me feel better. Their names were Rob and Cindy, and I was very thankful for them stopping. Gathering what strength I could, Rob and Cindy reluctantly watched me move towards town.

I barely made it to town and stumbled into the local gas station. A man with a badge approached me stating, "I've been getting calls for hours about you lying in the ditch." I thought to myself, "Well, where the heck were you when I needed you!" The deputy then asked if I was on drugs.

In a monotone voice, I simply stated that I was sick. While the cop was questioning me, Todd (the owner of the place) brought me some cold water. The officer's attitude completely changed to the positive and he offered to call an ambulance. Refusing medical help, Todd warned that he had to be packed in ice for heat exhaustion while in the Marine Corps, and urged me to get medical help.

The officer took me next door to the county jail and let me take a cool shower. He then fed me, and I took a nap in the air-conditioned lobby. Feeling a little better, I made camp behind the courthouse to rest a few days. Todd helped out considerably with well needed supplies. After three days of rest, I moved on.

The day I left Murphy, ID, a large bicycle race was passing through. The race was from Portland, Oregon, to Florida. Several camera crews passed by and filmed me. They all gave me a big cheer as they passed by. A local reporter stopped to ask why I was pulling a canoe in the race. After explaining that I wasn't in the race, the reporter quickly wrote down the story and moved on.

Days later, riding into the city of Mountain Home, I was beaten half to death with gravel. For several hours, dozens of semi-trucks loaded with gravel passed by at 60mph with their loads uncovered. Hearing an approaching truck, I would ball up the best I could to prepare for impact. Bloody and bruised, I finally passed the job site, located near the Air Force base.

My tires were getting bald again, so I purchased two more tires in Mountain Home, and replaced the badly worn break pads at a local bike shop. Leaving Mountain Home, I portaged back up into the mountains, leaving the hot valley below. Atop the mountain, taking a break, some travelers told me a woman on a bike was coming up the road.

Top 10 Meals of the Journey:

1. Ramen Noodles w/Ranch Style Beans
2. Peanut Butter & Jelly Tortilla Wraps
3. Macaroni & Cheese
4. Breakfast Cereal w/Powdered Milk
5. Canned Refried Bean Burritos
6. Snicker Bars
7. Sardines & Crackers
8. Plain Oatmeal
9. Fast Food Cheeseburgers
10. "Power Pancakes" (Pancake mix w/powdered eggs)

Instead of being a woman, it was a man. His name was John, a fellow adventurer; he had been bicycling around the world for the last two years. He had been through Southeast Asia, Africa and North America, and was now on his way home to end the trip somewhere in the Dakota's. We shared lunch and parted ways.

In Carey, Idaho, I spent a few days with the friendly locals. Pat, the owner of a RV Park, let me stay for free.

On up the road was Craters of the Moon National Park. Just inside the park boundaries, a support on my portage cart snapped under all the weight. I found myself stranded literally in the middle of nowhere. Not two minutes had passed, when a woman in a pickup, pulling a flatbed trailer, pulled up and offered me a ride. In complete disbelief of the fortunate opportunity, I accepted.

The miles seemed to fly by, and in no time Jean dropped me off in front of an automotive repair shop, where a mechanic named Jim welded it for free. Thanking God and Jim, I made camp a block away at a local campground.

Thirty miles north of Idaho Falls, at a vehicle inspection station, I met three crazy guys riding bicycles across America. One of them was pulling a small trailer that had a tuba in it. They had already heard about me in Carey, and wanted to know more about the adventure. After sharing stories, Scott pulled out his tuba and played the theme song from the Peanuts cartoon. Their group moved on to get a few more miles in for the day.

I made camp that night at the vehicle inspection station after getting permission to do so. The next morning, I awoke to my tent being flooded by an automatic sprinkler. I drug my tent away from the water's reach and lay back down to get some more sleep.

No sooner than closing my eyes, somebody backed a loud car to within two feet of my tent and revved up the engine, spilling exhaust fumes into the tent. I bailed out of my tent ready to fight, until I saw the badge pinned to the man's uniform. He was a vehicle inspector coming in for the morning shift. Looking around the large *empty* parking lot, I knew he had intentionally parked close to my tent just to annoy me. Giving him a dirty look, he laughed, and then went inside. I packed up my wet gear and headed out.

I reached the Continental Divide two days later. At over 7000 feet above sea level, I thanked God for bringing me so far. All waters from here lead to where I wanted to be most, home.

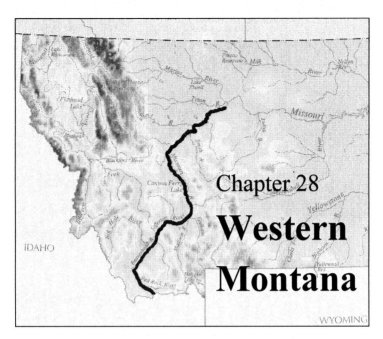

Chapter 28
Western
Montana

June 27 – July 20, 2002

Just over the divide was the town of Monida, MT. I found a payphone and called my family and friends to tell them of my progress.

Breaking camp from Monida, I rode 16 miles to Red Rock Creek, the upper most headwaters of the Missouri River. A local rancher gave me permission to put in on the creek, but warned of fences and diversion dams below.

Seeing that it was suicide to put in, I rode on toward Clark Canyon Reservoir. Leaving the blacktop highway, I utilized a gravel back road. Not far down, I discovered a huge bull had gotten out of the fence. It snorted and hoofed the ground acting as though it would charge. I stood my ground and the bull soon turned away.

Not even a mile further, I was stopped in my tracks by a large herd of cattle blocking the road. I took to the ditch and filmed the people on four wheelers herd the cattle. Two miles further and I made camp on the banks of Red Rock Creek.

The next morning my spirits were high as I put in and drifted along with the current. Soon the creek opened up to Clark Canyon Reservoir. Paddling out onto the open water, the lake was as smooth as glass. An hour later the wind began to blow, producing large whitecaps that pounded against the side of my canoe.

I turned away from the wind as my canoe began to take on water. Two hundred yards from shore, I paddled hard trying to keep myself positioned between the growing waves. Reaching shore, I surfed a large wave in, landing on the edge of a gravel beach. Another large wave crashed over me from behind as I hit shore. Jumping out, I was able to drag the half filled canoe up out of the water just as the next wave came crashing in.

The place I found myself marooned was significant in Lewis and Clark history. Buried at the bottom of the lake was Camp Fortunate, the very place Lewis and Clark stopped their ascent and began their historic portage over the Rocky Mountains. This was also where Sacagawea was reunited with her brother. The irony for me was this was my turning point from portaging to following the water home.

Still stranded the next day due to strong winds, I realized the lakes were going to be more of a problem than first anticipated. Eventually the wind subsided and I was able to finish paddling across the lake.

Utilizing a Jeep trail, the portage around the dam was completed with little difficulty. I put the canoe back in below the dam at the headwaters of the crystal clear Beaverhead River. Several guided drift boats were launching for a day of trophy trout fishing. One of the guides warned of some rapids to be found downstream.

My first day on the upper Beaverhead River offered majestic wild scenery consisting of mountains, bluffs and waterfalls. After an eventful day of running rapids on the beautiful clear river, I made camp at Barrets Dam Recreation area. Mountain goats dotted the tall mountain bluffs that towered above my camp.

The next morning I portaged around the dam and moved on. The river split off in several directions as it fingered itself around many small islands. Along this stretch of river I saw eagles, deer, moose and a lot of trout traversing the meandering river into Dillon, Montana.

Just passed Dillon, as the sun set, a man walked up to my camp and told me I had to leave. I told him, "In over 6000 miles you're the first to tell me to leave."

He went on to say he knew the landowners and that they would make me leave and threatened to call the police. It was almost completely dark, and clouds of mosquitoes hovered around my tent. I told him I wasn't leaving unless the landowner or the police insisted. I was below the flood line on a navigable stream, which makes for legal camping in most parts of America. The angry man stomped off through a cloud of mosquitoes and nobody else bothered me the rest of the evening.

The lower Beaverhead was so twisted that it was rare to see more than 50 yards of river before the next bend. The lower section of the river drastically contrasted the upper. Water quality was poor with a lot of cattle wading in it. Meandering through open prairie in view of mountains, I was continually pestered by clouds of mosquitoes. The water was murky and moved with schools of fish. Other wildlife included waterfowl, cranes, deer and muskrat.

It was a Fourth of July I wouldn't soon forget. Several diversion dams and fences crossed the lower Beaverhead River. Approaching one fence in particular, I pulled up and hopped out of the canoe into the river. Lifting the wire fence up to allow the canoe under, I found it to be charged with electricity.

Lit up like the Fourth of July, I forced myself loose. This was the first electric fence over water I had ever even heard about, let alone been shocked by. After cursing at the nearby farmhouse, I found a sturdy dry stick and lifted the wire and slipped under. Fences crossed the river every mile or so until near Twin Bridges.

The visible wildlife activities along this stretch of river helped shake off some anger. Mama ducks, at the sight of me, would quack to her babies and immediately they would take cover. She then would act wounded to lure me away. Sometimes the mama would go as far as a quarter mile "luring" me away.

Once while "luring" me away, a mink attacked her ducklings. Quickly she deserted me and attacked the mink. After several wallops on the head, the mink retreated.

I met several great people while awaiting mail in the small town of Twin Bridges. A rancher, named Johnny, I met there took me out to eat with his family and then out to his ranch. I helped him with some chores that included, milking his Jersey cow and freeing some of his sheep that were caught in the fence.

Walking around town, I met several of the townspeople. A man named Glen took me to his place of business. The small factory is nationally known for building high quality bamboo fly rods. He gave me a brief summary of the shops operations during the tour. Just as I was leaving town, I met a family riding cross country on a four-seater bike.

Just downstream from Three Bridges, the river changed again. At the confluence of the Jefferson River, the water turned clear and the river bottom changed from mud to potato sized stones. The river current was fast, but had no major rapids. It was one of the more beautiful rivers I'd ever seen, and the scenery only improved entering Jefferson Canyon. I found a nice gravel bar to camp on near the mouth of it.

Early the next morning I awoke to a kayaker coming down river. The sun was still behind the mountain as thick fog rose off the water. With chill in the air, I watched him pass by from my sleeping bag. It was like I was dreaming while being awake. Not wanting to waste a perfect morning, I got up and started coffee.

Soon the fog lifted and the river called me to move on. Inside the canyon, I spotted a large cave entrance. Beaching the canoe I grabbed my video camera and flashlight to go explore.

Rock climbing up the side of a bluff, I found it to be a mine instead of a cave. Several shafts led off into the darkness. The tunnels showed signs of instability where ceilings had become floors. Seeing too much potential danger, I turned around and went back to the canoe.

The bluff lined Jefferson periodically opened up into wide valley terrain in view of the snowcapped Rocky Mountains. Before long, Tosten Dam forced me into a half-mile portage in 100-degree heat before continuing. The summertime heat didn't bother me while I was on the river. At anytime I could beat the summertime heat and make progress by floating in the cool water along side the canoe, allowing the river to do the work.

One thing I observed different along this river was the behavior of birds of prey. Instead of perching high above the river, they hung out only a foot or two above it. Some would stand on the rocky bank, while others clung to root wads suspended above the water. Most of them had no fear at all of me, even at only a few feet away.

I soon arrived at Three Forks, Montana. It got the name from the three rivers that meet there. The Jefferson, Madison and Gallatin join to make up the headwaters of the Missouri River. A popular place for canoes to put in for an extended float trip, I was not alone. Several people I met had been paddling for at least a week.

Canyon Ferry Lake was the first major reservoir to cross on the Missouri River. Several people warned how the lake was very dangerous. Like all large lakes, in only a few minutes the calm waters could be transformed into deadly whitecaps.

The lake was like glass all day in the 100-degree heat; there wasn't even a breeze. Taking advantage of the smooth paddling conditions, I was able to cross most of the lake in one day. After 22 miles of paddling, I made camp. That evening, a black tail deer walked up to within five feet of me. Reaching out, it almost let me pet it, but then slowly turned and walked away.

The next morning, I reached the dam and prepared to portage. Within minutes of my landing, the wind began to blow creating large waves capable of swamping larger boats than mine. I had made it across the lake just in time. It was an eerie feeling, looking out over the frenzy of waves.

With the portage completed, the current was behind me again. Only a couple of miles through canyon terrain, the current slowed and the canyon opened up to Hauser Lake. The scenery was beautiful. Tall pine trees surrounded the small lake giving the air a fresh clean smell. Kids were jumping from the bluffs lining the lake to cool off in the clear cold water.

The river section below Hauser Dam was mind blowing. Pine covered mountains rose straight up from the river's edge. Trout feeding on the surface only added to the awesome scenery. The lake opened up for a short distance, but soon became a narrow canyon again. This canyon, known as Gates of the Mountains, consisted of 1200 feet of white bluffs dotted with tall pines.

It was the weekend and several boaters were out and about. Seeing my heavily loaded canoe, several asked, "Going all the way?"

My response was the same to all, "Just to Kansas City." Several boaters offered me food and cold drinks.

Sitting outside my tent watching the sunset, something felt weird. It donned on me that there were no mosquitoes. During a lot of the trip at this time of day, it was necessary to hide in my tent from the swarms of mosquitoes. I also observed a herd of elk grazing the mountainside a short distance away.

The next day, I portaged Holter Dam and put the canoe back into the clear flowing Missouri River. The swift current behind me made miles fly by. That night I was awakened to what sounded like a bear and a mountain lion fighting, just across the river. My guess was they were fighting over a fresh kill. I did not rest easy that night.

Two days out of Great Falls, MT, I was digging a cat hole and broke my paddle. Heart broken, I refused to give up on the paddle that had brought me so far. More to the point, my spare paddle was pretty much useless. I duct taped it back together and paddled on into Great Falls.

After giving away my bike to some people I met, five dams were now my obstacles. Utilizing a river trail, I found a Lewis and Clark Interpretive Center. Touring the center was very educational and a must see for anyone interested in Lewis and Clark history. A gentleman who worked there told me the trail ended not far away. He then shuttled me around the last two dams. Before leaving Great Falls, my Aunt Karen told me she would order and send a new paddle just like the one I had broken.

Putting back in below the lower dam of Great Falls was a sign stating, "Dangerous Rapids Ahead". The rapids consisted of 2-3 ft drops and 3-4 ft standing waves. Running them with a broken paddle was not going to work, so I ended up lining the canoe down most of them.

The river became peaceful below the rapids, with tall bluffs lining the river. Just outside of Fort Benton, I spotted several paddlers enjoying the river and paddled into town with them.

Fort Benton is considered the "Birthplace of Montana." The town was the last stop for paddleboats ascending the Missouri River - making it a very important depot for Western Expansion. The National Historic Landmark attracts history buffs and paddlers looking for a glimpse of America's past in a pristine landscape.

In historic Ft. Benton, I camped under the Lewis and Clark Memorial Statue at the river's edge and awaited the arrival of my new paddle. Touring the sites in town was fun and educational. I toured the river walk and museum after visiting several outfitter companies.

After returning to camp, I began to organize my gear. From behind me I heard somebody yell, "You ain't no paddler!"

Turning around, there was Robert videotaping me as he floated to shore.

Chapter 29

Missouri River Home

July 22 – September 13, 2002

My paddle arrived the next day General Delivery at the local post office. After another quick walk around town gathering last minute supplies, we packed up camp and prepared to leave. On our way back to the water, we met a reporter for the local newspaper and gave a quick interview.

Robert and I had heard about the Missouri Breaks for years and were anxious to get started. The next 149 miles of beautiful river were designated a National Wild and Scenic Riverway. Three to four hundred foot bluffs lined the Missouri River. Wild rock formations, resembling huge mushrooms, cover the hillsides. We saw several paddlers soaking in the scenery.

Hiking up into several side canyons for a change of pace, we found several fossils. We took several pictures and video of our finds and left them to return later and see again.

At camp one evening Robert built a power box. He took a cooler given to him back in California and taped a solar panel to the lid. He then put a car battery inside and secured it with duct tape. He cut a small hole in the lid with his pocketknife for the wires and attached a car stereo under the seat. An antenna was mounted to the stern of the canoe, which doubled as a flagpole. Two boom box speakers, given to him back in Idaho, were free to be placed anywhere. He also had a small inverter that was used to charge our video equipment batteries.

We were told at the put-in that drinking water was available along the route. Halfway through the section, we pulled up to a concessions store to get water. We went inside and discovered they charged $1.50 per gallon for tap water. They did not accept debit cards and Robert and I had only $4 in cash between us. We planned to just drink the river water instead of spending what little cash we had left.

Some people sitting outside, who had just taken off the river, heard the conversation inside and insisted that we take their left over drinking water. With our jugs filled, we headed downstream.

A lot less people used the Lower Breaks and we pretty much had the river to ourselves. Conifers and cottonwood trees lined the banks. Occasionally bighorn sheep could be seen grazing along the hillsides.

At the last take out of the Missouri Breaks, we met a group of vacationers taking out. Their river guide gave us a bunch of food and a box of wine. We spent the later half of the day floating along side our canoes, drinking wine and listening to Robert's radio. We still managed 50 miles for the day.

Two days later, I started the morning with a big rattlesnake coiled up under my canoe. The snake was only a foot away from my sandaled feet. Several days travel from any medical care, it gave me a good scare. I moved it aside with my paddle to a safe distance and we continued our journey home, paddling out across the upper reaches of Fort Peck Lake.

Just getting onto the lake was a challenge. Silt had accumulated due to the dam below, making the river only a couple inches deep.

Crawling on our hands and knees, we drug our canoes over the four-foot deep mud, for several hundred yards. The stinking mud created a vacuum with each step, forcing us to take several breaks before eventually reaching deeper water again.

The river widened even more and the current completely vanished. We rounded a corner and came upon an amazing sight. There on the opposite shore stood a herd of buffalo, numbering easily over one-hundred.

> **HERD OF BUFFALO**
> N 47° 28.265'
> W 107° 52.238'

A severe thunderstorm forced us ashore to take shelter. Fifty to sixty mph winds hammered us in a torrential downpour of rain. After the storm passed, a rainbow appeared over the herd of grazing buffalo. We grabbed our video equipment to catch the truly amazing sight.

Due to windy conditions, Ft. Peck Lake took much longer to cross than we ever anticipated. Windy every day, we only had an hour or two each day that we could paddle. Several days we were wind bound due to the ocean-size waves that covered the lake.

Being wind bound wasn't always bad. It gave us a chance to hike and explore the fossil covered hills surrounding Fort Peck. Looking up at the foothills when the light was right, it appeared that they were covered with diamonds. This was due to the large quantity of quartz crystals found in the area.

At Hell Creek Marina we met a nice couple from California who ran the place. They put us up in a room for the night at a discounted price. They also told us about a large camp set up for a T-Rex dig, just up the road.

Robert and I were introduced to Jack Horner. It was a true privilege to sit down and talk with a paleontologist legend. He took time out from his busy schedule and showed us some of the T-Rex teeth dug from the site. Around that same time frame, they uncovered a shocking discovery; actual pliable tissue from an extinct T-Rex.

After 18 days, and only 150 miles later, we finally crossed Fort Peck Lake. We met Bill, Chance, and Levi from Nebraska who were on a vacation fishing trip. They loaded us down with MRE's (Meals Ready to Eat) and sodas after helping us portage the Fort Peck dam. The earth filled dam was the largest in the world.

Fort Peck Lake was marked as a wildlife refuge, but we didn't see much wildlife on the lake. Below the dam, back on the river, wildlife could be seen everywhere. The water was clear and cold below the dam. Hundreds of ancient buffalo bones stuck out of the river bottom everywhere we looked.

Eight miles below the dam entered the Milk River from the north. The water turned murky again and picked up momentum.

Two nights later we were awakened by a terrible storm. Strong winds were snapping large trees as lightning and heavy rain came down all around. The storm went on as I tried to get some sleep. Around 5 a.m. I awoke to Robert screaming, "Jared get up!" Water was rushing into my tent from above and below.

Jumping out of my tent into the rain, I discovered that the river had flash flooded. Robert had already begun stuffing his soaked gear into dry bags and loading his canoe. Immediately, I followed suit. As we moved to higher ground in the pitch darkness, the rain tapered off to a drizzle. We drank some coffee and by 6 a.m. we were headed down the flooded river by first light.

Still mostly dark, we were wet, cold, and covered with mosquitoes. Signs of the ferocious storm could be seen everywhere as we rode down the flooded river. Large snapped off trees drifted along side our canoes. The debris posed an occasional threat when it collided into the sides of our boats. The sound of collapsing banks echoed all around.

One large bank had washed away taking dozens of trees along with it. The trees had created massive rapids spanning almost the entire width of the river. Several of the trees were sticking up through the dangerous rapids. Quickly maneuvering to a safe place to run the rapids, we slid through to safety. I remembered One-Eyed-Jack on the lower Missouri River warning us, "This River's a killer, I'm tellin' ya, a killer!"

The flooded waterway enabled us to make great time. Thunderstorms became almost a daily routine. Still nothing was worse than the mosquitoes and gnats. Even covered in 100% deet, mosquitoes attacked us by the hundreds. Gnats only attacked one area of the body—the eyes. Dozens of gnats died in our eyes each day. The river conditions in Eastern Montana were nothing short of miserable.

The radio warned of people contracting the West Nile Virus. Both of us were sick and weak, suffering from all the symptoms. Migraine headaches, fever, and nausea left us unable to paddle with much enthusiasm.

Finally making it to the confluence of the Yellowstone River, we set up camp next to a boat ramp on the north side of the river. Fishermen at the ramp warned us of the conditions down river—low water, lots of silt, and considered not navigable. Robert and I finally reached our breaking point and had enough of the lakes. After setting up camp, I put Robert's mountain bike together and rode over 20 miles into town to rent a U-Haul.

Three hours later, I was back and we loaded everything into the rental truck and drove around the lakes of North and South Dakota. Driving straight through, we arrived in Yankton, South Dakota at 3 a.m.. We found the public boat ramp and spent the rest of night in the back of the rental truck.

At daybreak, we unloaded the truck, I threw the mountain bike in the back and drove to the nearest U-Haul terminal. I peddled back to the river, loaded up and paddled away entering another beautiful Wild and Scenic section of the river. Daily headwinds slowed our progress, but we couldn't help but smile knowing that home was within 400 miles.

Sioux City had a lot of recreational boat traffic. Most of the people were friendly, offering us food and drink. Like most cities along the Lower Missouri River, pollution was present.

Down river we came to Cottonwood Marina where we were greeted with open arms. The owner, Mag, put us in a cabin for the night and Duane treated us to a large T-bone supper.

The Missouri River was known for some of the most generous and considerate river people, but we found none in Omaha, Nebraska. Boys in expensive toys tormented other river users everywhere we turned. One inconsiderate boater buzzed us at over 50mph, within four feet of me. I could have reached out and touched their boat with my paddle. The wake nearly threw me from the canoe, but I was able to prevent capsizing.

Robert cussed and gave every hand gesture trying to persuade them to stop. We wanted nothing more than to get our hands on the driver of the boat. Robert got the whole incident on video. Looking at the video at camp that night, I realized how lucky I was to have not been killed by the drunken boater, who was showing off in front of his friends.

We found a trend in our journey. Whenever times seemed to be at their worst, something good was just around the corner. Arriving in Brownsville, Nebraska we met Randal and Jane, who ran a riverboat tour company. They took us grocery shopping and for a tour of the historic river town. While preparing to leave, they invited Robert and me back for one of their fine dinner cruises aboard their riverboat.

Beautiful rolling hills covered with trees lined the river. Two days from Brownsville, we made it into our home state of Kansas.

Friday, the 13th of September 2002, we saw the tall skyscrapers of downtown Kansas City, Missouri. We paddled under several bridges and landed at Berkley Park, our original starting point. Our families greeted us as a local TV news crew recorded the moment.

Looking over the river, we looked downstream to where we had left and upriver from where we had returned. Of all the people, places and things we saw, "There's no place like home."

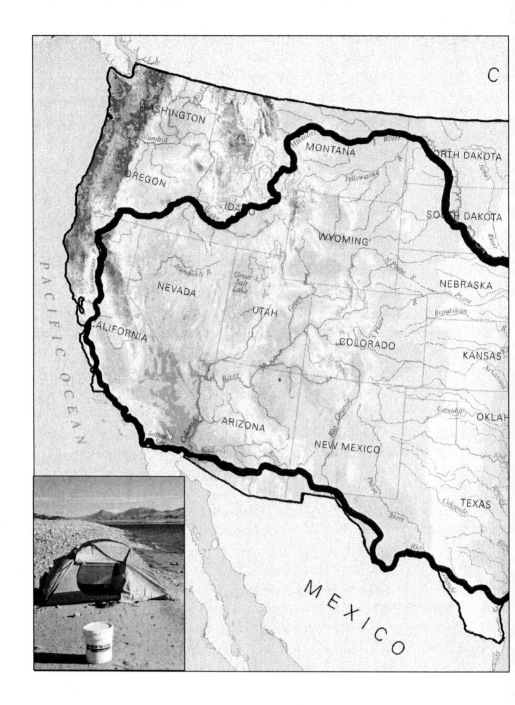

Map of the Route

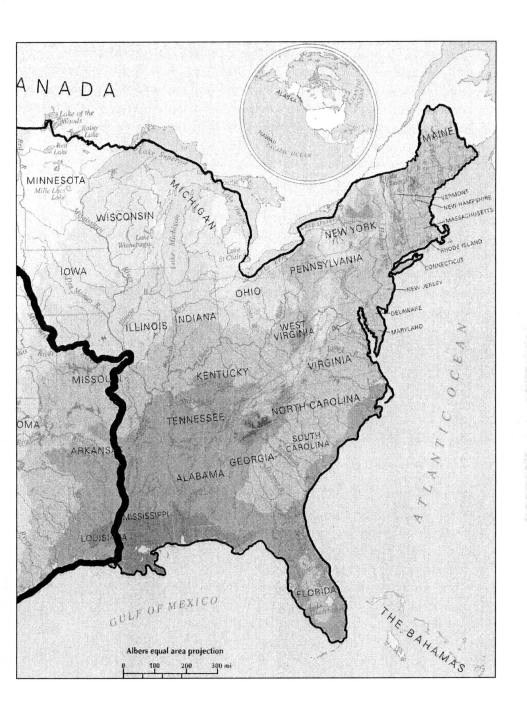

After the Journey

Robert and I both returned to Texas' Big Bend area and worked as river guides on the Rio Grande. While working that season, I stopped at a favorite local lunch spot and met LaNetta, the girl of my dreams. I later discovered that she was the originator of the "Alter Ego" party (chapter 18).

When the spring river season ended, I continued working as a river guide on the Arkansas River in Colorado. I quickly realized that paddling people down dangerous rivers was not my calling and joined LaNetta, who had moved to southern Colorado. Returning to construction, I worked on log homes, which was a new experience for me. After a couple of months, we moved to Tonganoxie, Kansas, not far from my hometown. I was very happy to be close to my family again.

I found employment as a painter and eventually we moved to The Lake of The Ozarks, Missouri, and bought a house overlooking the dammed up Osage River. The Lake is conveniently located within a short driving distance of many clear water Ozark streams. We float and fish as frequently as possible – whenever work and weather will allow.

The journey has given me a new perspective on life in general. At the time of this printing, I had started my own construction company and was happily working for myself. Robert and I have "parted ways" again as our lives took different paths. Last I heard, he was living in Branson with his fiancée, Cindy.

Unable to overcome my wanderlust, I continually dream of new adventures exploring unfamiliar destinations. I am often asked what the next adventure will be. The answer is always the same, "You never know what tomorrow brings!"

Acknowledgements

Thank you to God; My parents Larry and Julia Jellison; Helen Shewey; Karen Edelman; Sandie Runyon; Kenneth and Mary Lou Carpenter; Pete and Sandra McKaskle; Doug, Debbie, Chad, and Brody Young; Ian Kean (for the generous cash donation); Patricia Thomson; Alex Dugas; Douglas H. Chadwick; Jim Nelson; Phil Zinske; Shannon and Emerald; the people of Curly's World; Carlos and Whitey; Brad Gerber; Kurt Sindorf and Cal-Trans; and the many Law Enforcement agencies, Park Rangers, and Water Patrolmen along the way.

A special thanks to the countless generous people who helped along the way.

To all the people who thoughtfully and patiently help launch this book, thank you.